Members On

Ted Harrison is the former BBC Religious Affairs
Correspondent, now working as a freelance
broadcaster and writer. Married with two children
and two grandchildren, he lives near
Sittingbourne, Kent. This is the tenth book he has
written since 1977. His other titles include
Commissioner Catherine, *The Durham
Phenomenon*, *Much Beloved Daughter* (the story
of the first Anglican woman priest), and *Kriss
Akabusi On Track*. His most recent book was
about the Elvis Presley cult.

MEMBERS ONLY?

*Is the church Becoming
Too Exclusive?*

TED HARRISON

TRIANGLE

First published 1994
Triangle
SPCK
Holy Trinity Church
Marylebone Road
London NW1 4DU

British Library Cataloguing-in-Publication Data
A catalogue record for this book is available from
the British Library.

ISBN 0-281-04709-X

Typeset by Inforum, Rowlands Castle, Hants
Printed and bound in Great Britain by
BPCC Paperbacks Ltd
Member of BPCC Ltd

Contents

Acknowledgements   vi

Introduction—Rites for All?   1

1 The Sacred Place   13

2 'And Also with You'   28

3 'I'm the Vicar, Call Me Tim'   43

4 Forgive Us, Lord, for We Have Synod   63

5 Heritage and the New Folk-Faith   86

6 The Ordination of Women   102

7 A Church for the 'Unchurched'   112

*Appendix: The Results of the
Questionnaire*   127

Books Used for Further Reading   137

Acknowledgements

I am very grateful to the 300 clergy who took part in my survey and gave of their time and ideas, answering a lengthy list of assorted questions.

My thanks go, too, to Professor Robin Gill who kindly gave me guidance in compiling the questionnaire. The interpretation of the answers, however, is all mine.

My very special thanks go to my daughter, assistant, and general organizer, Caroline Harrison, for all her work in helping me write this book.

Introduction—
Rites for All?

Are the established churches in Britain fast shedding their role as churches for all, and merely becoming denominations?

This book is designed to explore that question, and I have set out to find some provocative answers. Indeed, in many ways, I have deliberately overstated some of my findings and impressions to stimulate debate.

For many years I have had the impression that the established Church of England—and, in some ways, the established Church of Scotland, too—are in danger of losing an essential purpose and contact with the people by, frankly, becoming too 'Christian'.

This may sound like an extraordinary thing to say, so perhaps I should explain myself. Christendom is made up of numerous groupings—ranging from the huge, to the ridiculously small—of people who firmly believe that they have captured the essential meaning of the mystery of the Christian faith; that only they have the key to salvation, truth and the meaning of everything. Traditionally, the Church of England and, to a lesser extent, the Church of Scotland have been described as broad churches. They have been able to embrace a huge diversity of practice and theological interpretation. They have existed as organic entities, thriving on their internal tensions. In the Thirty-Nine Articles or, as in Scotland, in the tradition of Presbyterianism and reform and the Westminster Confession, the churches have presented a public set of basic requirements of practice and belief, yet little doctrine was enforceable and everyone who claimed membership of an established church did so on his or her own terms. Indeed, many nominal members have outrageously heretical views, yet do not want to sever their connections with the national church, and feel entirely comfortable within it.

As a professional observer of the religious scene in Britain for nearly twenty years, it has been my impression that the established churches are losing the broad base that has so far provided them with an invaluable ability to relate to the many millions of British people who might be members in name and allegiance, but are, in reality, 'unchurched'. More importantly, as a result of the changing nature of the established churches, the 'unchurched' are finding it increasingly difficult to find a spiritual resource for themselves in those churches.

More people go to church on a regular basis in Scotland than in England, yet neither country can claim more than 10 per cent of its population as frequent attenders. Even so, a Gallup poll published in June 1993 demonstrated that spirituality was *not* on the decline in Britain. It showed that most British people think faith is a good thing, pray at least once a week and rate God as moderately important in their lives.

A full 59 per cent admitted to getting down on their knees, and 34 per cent of them do it daily. A full 40 per cent of people believed in an anonymous spirit or force, while only 30 per cent believed in the personal, biblical God. The survey also showed that more people believed in the Devil and hell than they did fifteen years ago, but fewer believed in God and heaven.

Even if we bear in mind the warning that polls must be regarded with caution, the Gallup survey is significant in that it shows a considerable degree of spiritual awareness, albeit unfocused and hesitant. The poll is a snapshot of the faith of the population at large, but what of the regular churchgoers?

Increasingly I have noticed the established churches of Britain becoming the homes of individuals and particular groups who are aware of certainty and intolerant of doubt. It appears to me that more and more congregations and parish churches are made up of cliques of individuals strong in their own understanding of Christian certainty. They rejoice in their faith and, in the style of their own particular brand of Christianity, approach their worship with enthusiasm and zeal. They are eager for new people to join them, and for these new recruits to discover and adopt *their* way of expressing the love and hope of Christ. They want to include as many people as possible—but only if the newcomers are prepared to fit in with them.

There is a tendency, therefore, increasingly, for churches to be made up of exclusive worshipping groups. Other people—especially those of a general inquiring nature, with unspecific and unfocused spiritual needs, with a feel for eternity but no love of instant answers—do not find a place in these groups. Neither do the millions who look to the timeless reassurance of the churches at certain times of year or certain stages in life, but do not want to sign up as regular believers.

In the current Decade of Evangelism, however, it may be that membership of the Church of England, the Church of Scotland and the other churches and denominations in the British Isles will actually increase. There is evidence that the decline in church attendance witnessed most of this century has turned. In the diocese of London, church electoral rolls have risen three years in succession, with a corresponding increase in confirmations. In the 1992 edition of *Church Statistics*, church attendances in England are generally steady, with ordinations keeping up. In 1991, 575 men and 240 women went to selection conferences with a view to ordination, the highest number for 4 years. Of the 325 men recommended, 274 were selected for stipendiary ministry, and, out of 123 women recommended, 85 were to be stipendiary. Also, church attendances on a normal Sunday were 1 154 800. Communicants on an ordinary Sunday numbered 724 000, rising to 1 549 200 at Easter—up by 1 per cent on the years before.

There are thriving congregations—within and without the established churches—of young people who have found the answers to life. These congregations flourish as, in an age of easy transport, like-minded people collect together.

As welcome as this new growth might be, should the tendency towards exclusivity become too prevalent, it is possible, I would suggest, that it could badly damage the spiritual life of the nation. It might lead to the complete breakdown of the parish structure. If this were to happen, then a notion that has been part of British spiritual life for a thousand years or more would be lost. This notion is that everyone, whatever their interest or lack of interest in religion, has a parish church to which he or she can go, and that everyone is included geographically within a congregation.

Maybe this has already happened to some extent in that the church, more and more, seems to be catering for 'Christians' only. Anyone who cannot, in all conscience, sign on the dotted line of a specific brand of Christianity may well find that they are not accepted. How different this is to William Temple's famous description of the church as a unique institution in that it exists for the benefit of those who are *not* members.

The present Archbishop of Canterbury, George Carey, echoed some of these concerns when speaking at Swanwick in Derbyshire at a conference on the gospel in culture in July 1993. He warned against fervent Evangelicals hijacking the Church of England's Decade of Evangelism.

> The church could so easily settle for easy answers which will satisfy only those already convinced that the church is the Truth . . . my fear for this decade is that it may encourage the forces . . . which actually wish to erect fences of doctrine and discipline, leading to a sectarian fellowship of believers.

4

It could be argued, of course, that, ever since medieval times, when the Christians took over the pagan sacred places for their acts of worship they have been in a minority. Initially, there was a blending of the Christian ways and the old traditions in order to meet the general spiritual needs of the people. People from both traditions attended the same churches at the same times of year. They shared the same festivals and rites of passage. They were, in time, all at least nominally members of the one church. In practice, however, the old ideas survived in people's hearts and life-styles. Indeed, the evidence quoted by Professor Robin Gill in his book *The Myth of the Empty Church* suggests that, certainly a century ago, the supposed golden age of church attendance when everyone attended Sunday worship, was largely a false memory.

> Communions on Easter day represented 8.4 per cent of the population aged over 15 in 1885. They reached their highest point in 1911 at 9.8 per cent. A slightly wider category of 'Easter Communicants' was adopted from the 1920s, which included Communions made in Easter Week. On this basis, in 1928 the rate was still 9 per cent (or 8.5 per cent on the original basis). By 1960 it was still 7 per cent, but then it declined to 5.1 per cent in 1970, to 4.7 per cent in 1980, and to 4.1 per cent in 1988.
>
> The number of those being confirmed also declined sharply after 1960. In 1872 there were almost 121 000 people confirmed, representing an estimated 28 per cent of the population aged over 15. They too reached their highest point in 1911, with some 244 000 representing 38 per cent of those aged 15. By 1960 there were still 190 000 people confirmed, representing some 32 per cent. But after this point, and despite confirmands being drawn from a much wider age range, the sheer numbers dropped sharply to 113 000 by 1970, to 98 000 by 1980, and to 62 000 by 1989.

So, while the 'churched' might once have been double the number today, the total has always represented a minority of the population. The majority used the services of the church for weddings, funerals, and special occasions only.

Today, however, those who do *not* go to church, those who do *not* want to sign up for the 'Jesus movement' or the rituals of Catholicism, and do *not* want to belong to a worshipping fellowship, seek spiritual outlet in other ways. This can take many forms. For instance, people have direct access to the great music of our civilization, the music that reaches deep into the soul. What was once only available in church can now be heard on Classic FM every day of the week. Also, people can turn to a wide range of gurus and curious pagan revival faiths to feed their yearnings for answers to the eternal questions. It would be wrong to generalize, but there are a growing number of places in Britain where church life has retreated behind the walls of the church buildings and vicarages and consists of self-perpetuating and self-justifying cliques that only want members on their own terms.

This is an impression that has developed over many years and, when researching this book, I decided to check it out more systematically. I despatched a questionnaire to a wide, random sample of clergy in the Church of England. I have had a 60 per cent response rate, yielding some 300 detailed answers (see the Appendix, page 127, for the questions and responses). My hunches have been confirmed in many ways, but not in others. It seems that the church as spiritual centre for everyone, irrespective of confessed belief, survives, but generally only in rural areas. In such parishes, the picture is still recognizably the same as that which has existed for centuries, with a higher proportion of each congregation being drawn from the parish catchment area. More people in the rural areas remain nominal members of the national church than in the towns and, in all probability, have at the centre of their community a church building that dates back several centuries.

The urban Church of England, on the other hand, is now, by and large, just another denomination, with few claims to being the church for all people. In many cities, more people attend Roman Catholic masses on Sundays than go to worship in an Anglican church. Those that *do* choose the Anglican option overwhelmingly go to churches that meet their specific requirements rather than to the one in their immediate ecclesiastical parish. The church buildings are often relatively new and not built on ancient, sacred places. Also, the people living there do not have their roots in the district and so maybe this is why urban churchgoers feel free to 'shop around' as it were to find the particular type of worship they prefer.

The results of the survey do not necessarily apply to the established Church in Scotland, but inferences can be drawn.

As an aside, it was interesting to note, too, that, in general, figures for church attendance and membership gathered from the questionnaire were less optimistic than those gathered for official statistical purposes. In many cases churches stand as small islands in a sea of other faiths. For example, one clergyman contacted pointed out that in his parish the population was 80 per cent Muslim.

So, what do townspeople do if they just want their local church to be there for their occasional needs? Eager, smiling Christians on the one hand or the devotees of the minutiae of ritual on the other are both extremely off-putting types to the majority of people. I fear that what the townspeople do is use the undemanding services of the State—marry in register offices and dispose of their relatives at the municipal crematorium.

Yet, every member of this majority still has, at some stage in life, to face the essential spiritual questions—what is the purpose of life, what happens after death, why is suffering allowed? Human beings are spiritual beings, with the capacity to love and wonder. Human beings are also endowed with an intellectual capacity and many people shy away from instant, pat answers.

It would be as well for many who are members of the increasingly denominational Church of England to think on two quotes. One is from Lord Runcie, the former Archbishop of Canterbury, much reviled in his time for his ability to see both sides of an argument, but who, at a personal level, engendered much loyalty and affection. The other is from his wife. Rosalind Runcie first. On being questioned about her faith at the time of her husband's elevation to the See of Canterbury, she spoke for many thousands, if not millions of people, when she uttered the memorable words, 'Too much religion makes me go pop!' The quote from her husband is taken from an interview given right at the end of his time as Archbishop: 'The older I get, the more and more I believe about less and less.'

I feel it is only fair at this point to tell you something of my own religious heritage. I have been a member of the Church of England ever since a date in 1948 when, as a 'mewling and puking' infant, a sign of the cross was made on my forehead with water, and I was welcomed into the Christian family. My father was 'the vicar' and all my early life consists of memories of the church—its rhythms, its life, its responsibilities. In adulthood, I have reported on and studied the church professionally as BBC Religious Affairs Correspondent, presenter of the BBC radio programme *Sunday* and through my many years as a journalist specializing in religious affairs. Personally, I am something of a religious chameleon. I have felt at home in many places of worship. I have been to Pentecostal services, I have watched Orthodox rituals, I have been to mosques, temples, indeed, almost every type of place where God is worshipped. I remember sitting through one of the offices of the monks on the island of Patmos and feeling transported back in time. I have experienced cathedral evensongs at their best, worshipped in quiet country churches on dull wet Sundays, been to great State occasions, and joined small groups of members of religious orders in daily worship. While my work gives me little time to become an active member of a local congregation, I *have* spent time on an English parochial church council, although I cannot

8

think I contributed very much to the discussions about where and whether to site a lavatory in the church and who would run which stalls at the fête.

I have intruded on many moments of intense religious encounter experienced by others and witnessed some extraordinary things. I am convinced that the spiritual is an essential part of modern life, even in this material age and, yet, not being a clubby person, I am deterred from seeking too close an involvement in a worshipping community.

Normally I adopt an entirely objective approach when reporting on religious affairs. I stand back and take the dispassionate line. However, for the purpose of this book, I admit to blending my objective research with some of my subjective opinions. I admit, for instance, that I dislike some of the changes that have taken place in the Church of England, which, I believe, have contributed to the trend towards denominationalism. I suspect that the changes to the liturgy of the church and the introduction of the Alternative Service Book have been particularly damaging in this regard. The survey shows overwhelmingly that, in less than the span of a generation, the Book of Common Prayer has faded from general use. It has been replaced by the alternative liturgies that were introduced not, as one might suppose, solely to update the language of worship, but to strengthen worship as a congregational rather than an individual act and obligation. The compilers of the Book of Common Prayer never assumed that members of the Church of England would be a 'gathered' church. They did not think of them as the few committed Christians of the area coming together for fellowship and worship. Rather, they assumed that they were writing for everyone living in the parish, whoever they might be, obliging them only to attend church for Holy Communion three times a year. The Alternative Service Book takes a view of the congregation more in line with that of the Roman Catholic church following the Second Vatican Council; that the people of God worshipping together are to be sent out into the world with a commission to take with them the Christian gospel and demonstrate their faith by example.

This change in emphasis is justified by the changes in society. Modern Christians would argue that they are again, like their forebears in the early centuries after Christ, a minority. They are not persecuted by a hostile pagan world, but, nevertheless, feel themselves to be at odds with the secular age. Their aim is to reconvert the world.

Is this the goal they should pursue, though, especially if success is measured by the numbers of people persuaded to attend church on a regular basis? Maybe filling churches is *not* the first priority. It can be strongly argued that going to church and being part of a worshipping community is not essential in order to be a Christian. Indeed, there are many devout and holy people who quite deliberately pursue their own paths with only the occasional reference to others. There is, too, an historical tradition of hermits. Also, in the Church of England of years gone by, the 8.00AM Communion service on a Sunday morning catered for those who wished to pursue a path of individual devotion. They attended as part of their personal obligation to their faith, preferring not to be a member of a wider congregation, feeling that they would have to put on some act of false camaraderie and Christian jollity.

A national church, I believe, should be there to enable and encourage all people to develop a spiritual awareness and be a place to which anyone can turn for spiritual guidance. It is doing its job when it is readily accessible to all and not pushing a particular line. It is inconceivable that when Jesus went to dine with the taxpayers, prostitutes, and other sinners that he spent the time instructing them in how to keep to the detail of the Jewish law of the day. Instead, it was the experience of him that counted.

Today, that experience can often be best found outside the churches. Folk-faith and spiritual awareness are far more important driving forces for the individuals outside the church than are the church dogma, practices, and traditions found inside it. As the leaders of the established churches allow and encourage their churches to shed their role of being available to all, they would do well to remember the role of folk-faith and not think that their calling is to turn people into Christian clones.

What, after all, are the basic requirements for being a Christian? Every Christian knows, but, when it comes to explaining these basics in more detail, there is huge scope for division. The need for such explanations arises even when only particular elements are changed. For example, the Church of England is in quite a whirl regarding the debate about the ordination of women to the priesthood. There are those who say that the Church of England will split irreparably over the issue. However, similar warnings were made in Scotland not that long ago when this issue was debated there, but the church remains intact. Certainly, analysing the comments from the English clergy surveyed within the context of my own observations of the debate over twenty years, I would argue that the whole controversy is destined to be short-lived and unlikely to produce the dire consequences foreseen. I would suggest, too, that to those outside the church it is an unimportant, trivial argument of little relevance. In the secular world, there is very wide acceptance of women in positions of responsibility. Within the church context, I feel that the matter will be resolved within a generation or two if the Roman Catholic church accepts women as priests.

The *real* dilemma facing the Church of England, which will eventually threaten it with schism, is this. Here I quote from the opposing camps using the words of respondents to the questionnaire. First of all, a vicar from a large, rural parish in North Yorkshire with twenty-five years' experience of parish ministry:

> It is not clear how long a diminishing membership and ministry in the Church of England can go on caring for the 'unchurched' who require only baptisms, weddings

and funerals. Something will have to give. I would rather spend time building up the faithful than spend it burying the 'unchurched'. I favour disestablishment because it might force folk to 'opt in' to the Anglican Church rather than just assume they are members because they are British. The Church of England will become more confessional and less communal.

Now for a quite opposite view, expressed by the vicar of a large, urban parish in the St Alban's Diocese:

I very much hope that the church remains . . . a witness of its care for all those within the parish.

This view was echoed by a clergyman in his sixties with a large, rural parish in Wiltshire:

I believe the Church of England must stand by the parish system, i.e. to have a personal relationship and commitment to all who reside in these islands who are not otherwise committed. We are not a sect or congregational set-up and must not for reasons of convenience or financial difficulty or supposed lack of vocations become one either.

The Sacred Place

One hot summer's day, not that long ago, I had occasion to be in the churchyard attached to an old parish church in the New Forest. There were birds singing, bees moving from flower to flower and multicoloured butterflies flitting about. A slight, cooling breeze produced the barest whisper of movement in an old yew tree. It was one of those moments when one can truly think all is right with the world. I walked slowly round the church, oblivious of time. As I rounded the east end, I saw an elderly couple sitting on a wooden seat. I approached them and we passed the time of day.

Casual greeting turned into a conversation. The man, grey, lined and in his late seventies, wanted to talk. He told me that, at that very moment, his brother's funeral was taking place. Because his own health was not good, he explained that he and his wife were unable to make the 200-mile journey to be at the service. So, they had decided to come, at the appropriate time, to their local church and sit in the churchyard with their thoughts and memories. They were not regular churchgoers, he said (they went a couple of times a year, at Christmas and harvest-time) but, nevertheless, he felt that the church was his. He and his wife had been married there, had their children baptized there, and both expected that, one day, they would be buried together in the churchyard near to where they sat.

I learnt, too, that the man had lived a quiet, responsible life, with only the war years providing excitement and travel. His wife had always lived in the area and, except to visit family, they had seldom travelled far away. They had both seen many changes in their time, with new estates being built on fields near their home where, as children, they had played. The population of their community had at least doubled, perhaps trebled in the last twenty years. Cars, once a novelty, were now a nuisance.

He told me they now had television and central heating and were materially more comfortable than they had ever been. Like millions of others in Britain, they had benefited from the post-war years of prosperity. Yet, those benefits had a down side. None of their children could now afford to live locally, even if they could find work nearby. He and his wife only saw their family from time to time. The grand-children they barely knew, particularly as one son and his family were living in Australia.

As we spoke, it was never actually said but nevertheless acknowledged by both of us, that the man was nearing the end of his life. His health was not good and he would be making his acquaintance with death before too long.

He was a man with a faith, but no theology. His faith lay in his instinctive feel for the rhythms of life, for creation, for the Holy, and for the sacred place where he now sat.

Since their childhood, he and his wife had seen some changes at the church, too.

Once, the vicar had been a well-respected local figure. He had lived slightly apart in the grand old rectory, but he knew everyone in the community. He was addressed formally and returned the compliment. He had been in the post for such a long time that he baptized the children of those he had baptized twenty or so years before. He was also a man the community felt they could turn to in times of trouble. Families facing hard times could expect the vicar and his wife to rally round. Today, such kindly efforts would seem rather patronizing, but, in those days, it was accepted that they would find clothes and food for those in real need. People came to him with their troubles, family problems, in times of distress, death, family feud, and sadness. He made a point of being out and about in the village.

At even the rumour of illness, he would knock on a door to enquire how people were. He delivered, by hand, every one of the parish magazines produced once a month. He delivered birthday cards to the children he had baptized, called on newcomers to the village and was, simply, available.

His successor was much the same, but did not stay so long, and, since then, the couple in the churchyard recalled a succession of incumbents. More recently, the parish had been combined with another and all they saw of the vicar was a man in a dog collar driving past in a car. Today they could not even remember the new man's name.

The man in the churchyard said that these days he and his wife very seldom went to church. The people there were not people they knew; they were all newcomers. The order of service was new—it was always Communion and never matins. 'They even say the Lord's Prayer differently these days', he said. He and his wife had once ventured to the family service on an ordinary Sunday, but were embarrassed by a woman they had only sometimes seen around the village but never spoken to who grabbed each by the hand, which she shook warmly, 'quite unexpectedly, in the middle of the service'. Later, over coffee at the back of the church, 'not something the old vicar would have allowed', another woman had asked him if he wanted to join her prayer group and if he 'really knew Jesus'.

Relating that encounter with the elderly couple might appear to be taking too sentimental an approach to the past. Memories, of course, are notoriously unreliable. Pain and tedium are eliminated and golden ages created in the imagination. Yet, even allowing for the fallibility of the human mind, I was sure that there was a very real message in what the couple were telling me. While to them the new incumbent and his small congregation of enthusiasts were alien to their idea of what the Church of England should be like, they nevertheless had not rejected the idea of the importance of the church in their lives and in their community.

They had deliberately chosen to go to the churchyard at the time of a family funeral; to absorb the atmosphere of a sacred place, to re-root themselves in the mystery of the folk-faith that had comforted and sustained them from youth. For them it was the most appropriate thing to do.

Around them, as they sat there, were many gravestones. On these stones, undoubtedly, were the names of some of their own ancestors. All the changes that had taken place in the parish structure, to the Church of England liturgy, and organization, had taken place in little more than a decade. The church they knew, however, its virtually unchanged traditions and history, were rooted in centuries of English life. Indeed, the church itself was probably built on the site of an earlier place of worship where the pre-Christians of these islands had met to mark the seasons of the year and their rites of passage.

It is often assumed, wrongly, that England became a Christian country soon after Augustine arrived in Kent in 597 with his missionaries and converted Ethelbert, the local king. However, as the historian Henry Mayr-Harting wrote in his book *The Coming of Christianity to Anglo-Saxon England:*

> In spite of there being good political and cultural reasons for the conversion of kings to Christianity, in spite of an extraordinary galaxy of able and saintly missionaries, it took nearly ninety years to convert just the kings and the greater part of their aristocracy, not to speak of the countryside, which was a question of centuries. In the course of that near-ninety years, hardly a court was converted which did not suffer at least one subsequent relapse into paganism before being re-converted. The old religious instincts died hard.

There is strong evidence that these 'instincts' did not die out for many centuries and, possibly, new forms of paganism also took root *after* the arrival of Christianity. For example, visitors to the church at Wormshill in Kent will learn from the brief history of the village inside that the name derives from an older version, Woden's Hill. The official scribe of the 'Domesday Book', however, calls the place God's Hill, but, clearly, 500 years after Kent was officially converted to Christianity, this name was not in popular usage as it is the older form, dedicated to the pagan god, that has survived.

Further evidence that pre-Christian beliefs persisted well into the Christian age and even coexisted can be found in many hundreds of medieval places of worship. Legend has it that churches were shared by both groups, with the Christians entering by a south door and the pagans by one in the north wall. Today, a blocked entrance is a common sight in the north wall of churches 700 or more years old.

Other echoes of pre-Christian Britain still survive: Woden, for example, still gives his name to the middle day of the week. Christians even adopted the pagan midwinter festival to celebrate the birthday of Christ—a date for which there is no biblical or historical evidence. And it is on Christmas day when churches all over the country are most used. Although Easter is the only day stipulated in the Book of Common Prayer when members of the Church of England should take Holy Communion (it is also a day that can be fixed in the calendar according to biblical evidence), in the survey of clergy I conducted, Christmas services were said to be overwhelmingly better attended than Easter ones. Of nearly 300 replies, 69 per cent of parish clergy said that the Christmas service was the most popular one of the year, although, in some cases, it shared that position with the Remembrance Sunday observation, harvest festival or Easter day. The Christmas services described took varying forms, but mainly carol singing or Christingle services are popular. It was unusual, therefore, when the vicar of an urban parish in West Yorkshire, living on a housing estate with a reputation that he described as 'notorious within the metropolitan district with all the usual features of multiple deprivation', made the observation that, in his case, there was very little difference between the numbers who came to church at Christmas and Easter, but, he wrote, we have virtually no fringe of occasional churchgoers.' This observation tends to suggest that, in certain areas of social breakdown, the folk-faith of the nation has also disintegrated.

The survey in general, then, confirms that amid the commercialization of a modern Christmas, there is an impulse felt by many millions of people to gather at the turn of the year in an ancient building, on an ancient, sacred site, to re-enact a familiar, seasonal rite. Many people in the cities have a modern church or a Victorian replica of an older one, but that is not where they are in spirit. In spirit, they are in the stone village church of the Christmas card, in the sacred place of their forebears.

Indeed, to the couple I met, and many others like them, the place is as important as the worship inside. For example, a common difficulty experienced by many clergy when parishes have to be amalgamated and it is suggested that, in the interests of efficiency, services are sometimes held in one church and sometimes in another, is that parishioners are very reluctant to go anywhere but to their own, familiar building. Seldom is there hostility between congregations or rivalry, it is just that the other church, however near, is unfamiliar. Going to church—that essential time of quiet, worship, and communion with God—is associated in the minds of so many people with a familiar and much-loved building.

Maybe it is just British conservatism. Some Christians might even argue that it is a sign of a lack of real Christian commitment and faith that some people invest more emotion in the building than in the worship. Yet, it is a familiar pattern and one that the church needs to try and understand. This phenomenon occurs because, to many people, particularly in rural areas, although not necessarily exclusively so, these sacred places are the key to the fulfilment of their faith. Up and down the country, there are small, historic, out of the way churches that are of no special significance except to the local community, often kept going by as few as two or three dedicated souls. They give their time and offer their best to the church. Try as visiting preachers might to associate the word 'church' with 'the worshipping community', 'the body of Christ', and so on, inevitably, to the community, the church means the building, the stone structure built on a holy site.

I remember once visiting a small church in the West country that had become so dilapidated that it was being propped up by scaffolding. It had been the centre of worship for a thriving community for many centuries, but, as a result of social change and economic forces, the immediate parish congregation had dwindled to forty. That is, forty people living within the parish, not forty churchgoers. A few people from outside supplemented the congregation on Sunday, but, by and large, it was left to those forty to maintain a structure that needed tens of thousands of pounds spent on it, immediately. All their efforts were directed towards raising that money.

Some feared it was a hopeless cause—an outsider might have argued that it was a *pointless* cause—and, yet, the dedication was there, and sorrow and heartbreak would have been the result if the church had been closed.

There is plenty of evidence around England of the social changes that have forced many churches to close. Statistics show that, even during periods of great church-building, such as in the suburbs in the Victorian times, there were never enough people attending to fill all the pews. Churches were built of a size to cope with a maximum congregation and that maximum always included people from outside the parish. Inevitably, more church pew space was built than could possibly ever be needed. Constructing a large church was sometimes more a declaration of faith than a sensible provision of adequate covered space.

Today, a church is made redundant only as a last resort. Perhaps in the past, nature was allowed to take its course more freely—a journey through Romney Marsh in Kent is evidence of this. There are a number of ruined buildings that must have had thriving congregations at one time. Yet, even a ruined church can retain an aura of spirituality for those who visit. Indeed, many people would claim that a walk around a ruined monastic abbey is far more uplifting to the spirits than a walk around an old Roman villa, a place with no spiritual associations. Also, followers of the revived neo-pagan faiths in Britain like to seek out the ruins of former places of worship in which to conduct their seasonal or lunar ceremonies, so such feelings cannot be dismissed.

An ancient surviving church, however, is not just a place of meeting and worship, it is an object of witness. It stands there, saying to all the world that the church and the Christian faith is at the heart of the community. The church, certainly in every rural community, is the most conspicuous and visible building. It is invariably the tallest building and many have ornate spires and towers that dominate the landscape. As Nigel Nicolson wrote in *English Country Churches*:

> A church is the village hub. It is the first building that a child will set down in arranging a toy town; he or she will want it, instinctively, to be medieval, and when he or she marries, the older the church, the better. The church is our main link with the remote past.

While people whose ancestors have lived in the area for centuries have a special empathy with the building, the power of such sacred places is not lost on visitors either. To those travelling from city to city, the churches are landmarks. Whether seen from a train or a motorway, churches command attention. Small and picturesque or huge and cathedral-like, they punctuate the landscape and give it purpose.

To those travelling slowly, it is fascinating to journey around the countryside visiting old churches and, when they are open, an unfortunately rare thing these days, looking at the visitors' books. They are records of the feelings of the casual visitors who have called in, looked around, bought the postcard, read the handbook, admired the squire's tomb and the unusual pulpit, and then left something of themselves behind: 'So beautiful and peaceful', 'An inspiring place', 'I needed to come here just for a few quiet moments', 'An oasis of calm in the midst of stress.' Sometimes the messages are in a child's hand and the addresses given are just a few miles away. Often much longer messages are left, with the writer claiming a connection with the parish and giving an address in Canada or Australia. Whatever the literary merits of the messages, they all bear witness to an intangible something that even the most insensitive visitor derives from a church.

A country church is not like a cathedral with dozens of people milling around, official signs on display, the magnificence and opulence of a whole county on show. The parish church is the workhorse of English Christianity. It is a place that has seen all the joys and sorrows of the nation in microcosm. It is a place where the prayers of the faithful have, it seems, been absorbed by the stonework. There is that unmistakeable smell of stone, history, damp, flowers, and, at certain times of the year, harvest vegetables.

Perhaps behind a curtain in the corner is the vestry. With stored hymn-books, the old Ancient and Modern now seldom used, going white with damp. On the wall, the photograph of the bell-ringers in 1928, the captain of the team sporting a large walrus moustache. There might also be a delicate, sentimental 'gentle Jesus meek and mild' print for the children's Sunday school, a cupboard containing a candle snuffer, and enamel vases and jugs for the flowers. It is just this kind of accumulated detritus of Anglican worship that is familiar to so many. Yet the church is not a museum; it is still a place of worship. Would the bell-ringing team of barely seventy years ago recognize what is going on in that church today?

By the door there is now a thin paperback booklet containing the particular version of the Alternative Service

Book Communion service used. There will be a duplicated letter from the vicar, written in a chatty style, telling his congregation not only parish business, but his latest thoughts on the world situation. If the old bell-ringers were able to travel through time, they would not recognize the service; even the couple in the churchyard no longer know what is going on in the place with which they are so familiar.

It could, of course, be argued that this is how it has always been. When Hymns Ancient and Modern was first introduced, there would have been discontent. When the organ replaced the impromptu village band, there would have been dissent. When candles were first placed on the altar and vestments introduced, elderly parishioners would have protested that the church was veering towards Rome. To take an actual example, the bishop visiting St John's church, Torquay, in 1847 found that the local incumbent had introduced a number of items of decoration of which he strongly disapproved. These were a wooden cross decorated with flowers and evergreens and two small, glass flower vases. 'Seizing one of the vases', writes Peter Hammond in his book *The Parson in the Victorian Parish*, 'he pushed it off the altar.' However, the bishop was thwarted in his endeavour to rid the altar of its decoration as the vase, he discovered, was attached to the holy table by a string.

Could it be argued that there is one key difference between the changes of old and those of today? In the past, whatever the adaptations, it would have been unthinkable to abandon the church as a building. Today, when clergy and congregations are asked, which is most important, the worship or the building, they frequently answer 'the worship'. Would they perhaps be prepared to leave the church building, with all the attendant costs of maintenance, and hold their services in the village hall? Many say, 'yes'. I have not quantified these answers—I rely on my recollection of many conversations over the years—but that is my impression. I suspect that, through most of the history of the recent centuries, such a suggestion would not have even occurred to anyone, yet, today, there will be many newcomers to the parish and the faith (who make up the core of worshippers) who would argue strongly that, as beautiful as the building is, a church is no longer essential. Indeed, some would argue that the church building itself is actually a hindrance. First of all, it drains even quite wealthy parishes of resources, money better spent on social work at home or abroad, for example. Second, they would argue that it is not only too expensive to maintain, but too expensive to keep secure. Where only a few years ago it was possible for all country churches to be left open, today more and more have to be locked for reasons of security.

The argument might be augmented by the very convincing point that biblical sources would indicate that the preservation of ancient buildings is quite opposite to the intentions of Jesus. Yet, all these valid arguments miss a fundamental truth: what is stored up in a church is not a personal treasure, but a communal legacy. It is evidence of the faith of the past. The ancient stone reassures the present generation of regular churchgoers and occasional churchgoers alike that they are part of something rooted in history. Many medieval parish churches take the modern generation at least half-way back to the times of Christ. Also were not the buildings themselves constructed as acts of worship and, if so, is lovingly caring for a church not an act of worship?

Admittedly some, certainly in East Anglia, were built in a flurry of mercantile one-upmanship, as the wool merchants vied with each other to build the grandest structures. It is certainly the case that, in many parish churches, the grandest tombs are those of squires wishing to show their superior position in the community, but it does not take very much of a search to find real evidence of the dedication of the many over the centuries. Covering the walls, there are to be found small tablets commemorating the lives and giving thanks to God for the service of a church warden or an organist. There is the new pew or organ case or altar in the side chapel given in memory of someone who spent many years working for the church. Going back further, there are the delicate carvings, perhaps even wall paintings, that are the work of anonymous artists. Some of them will be naive and child-like, possibly evidence that a local artist created them rather than a touring professional.

Today, it is necessary to get a legal document in order to change anything inside a church under the jurisdiction of the Church of England. In the past it was left to the taste of the local congregation, the pocket of the squire, and the guidance of the incumbent to decorate the church architecture and otherwise contribute to its appearance. Interestingly, 68 per cent of the clergy surveyed found that by and large, the faculty regulations were acceptable. However, 27 per cent found them too strict, while a few pointed out that recent changes to church law had not been in force sufficiently long for judgements to be made. One respondent described church law as 'ridiculous', another called it 'stupid', and a third remarked 'we'll soon need a faculty to weed the graveyard!' However Christ himself would not have been unfamiliar with special care being taken to maintain the fabric of a holy place: building and keeping the temple in Jerusalem in good repair was very important to the Jews of his time.

The carpenter of Nazareth who, in the last three years of his life, lived an austere wandering, mendicant life had, as a boy and young man, regularly visited the places of worship dedicated to God. He knew the great temple and, although shocked by the commercialism of the outer courtyards, would no doubt have viewed the inner sanctum with reverence. He would have known his local synagogue and known that it had a special place in the affections of his fellow Nazarenes. He knew the role of the tabernacle—that place constructed, set aside, and dedicated to God. He would have known that, although on an intellectual level the people would talk of the universality of God, God being in everything and around everything, they had a need to concentrate their minds in a particular place. Also that, if that place has been used by generation after generation, it takes on a certain aura of its own that can inspire and stimulate the generations that follow.

A church of England that underestimates the importance of spiritual places is one that is undermining one of its own greatest strengths. Without its hundreds of parish churches and dozens of cathedrals, the Church of England would be an impoverished denomination. Indeed, a church and the sense of spiritual awe that the building can inspire can be a more powerful evangelical tool than any number of sermons and tracts. History can speak to people without words. The sense of peace and quiet that the visitors to old churches inevitably note in the visitors' books is of a special kind. The spiritual nourishment they derive from these quiet moments is indefinable. There is certainly a danger in the great cathedrals of undervaluing and defiling this effect. The commercialization, the organization of the visitors, the demands for money on entry, insensitive, bossy vergers, and the way many cathedrals are run as heritage centres, all detract from—even destroy altogether—the very thing that people coming to these places are looking for.

Canterbury Cathedral is the one I know best. When I was very young, my parents lived in Kent and we visited Canterbury from time to time. On these occasions we always visited the Cathedral. I got to know the Black Prince's tomb, the place where Becket was murdered, and the ghost story told about the spooky Dark Entry into the cloisters. Later, I lived in Canterbury for three years when I was a student and I never visited the centre of the city without going to the Cathedral. It is at its best either early in the morning in winter, when few people are around and one can wander through, hearing one's own footsteps on the stone, or at some great occasion, when the Cathedral is packed and the choir is singing. To visit at any stage in between is to be disappointed. Worst is to go to the Cathedral at the height of summer in the afternoon when the coach parties have disgorged their occupants and the Cathedral is milling with rowdy French school children. Also, while I like to put some money into one of the boxes, I dislike being 'blackmailed' into giving money when I enter and want only a brief wander round.

Other cathedrals deal with the problems of peak demand in different ways. Some are even more demanding of people's money. In some, the cathedral officials are officious to the extreme. In one very well-known cathedral, I remember sitting listening to evensong and sensing nothing of any value from it at all; the professional choir and paid canons seemed as if they were going through some tedious ritual.

The impact, though, of the buildings now in the care of the Church of England is far wider than their immediate legacy of prayer or the benefits that can be derived by visitors from the quiet moments inside them. The church has infiltrated the geography of these islands. In Wales it is quite obvious as almost every village is called 'Llan' something and, thus, directly takes its place name from the church in its midst. In England, hundreds of places are named after the saints to which their cathedrals are dedicated, such as Bury St Edmunds and Peterborough, to name two cities, or other places like St Peters in Thanet. Throughout London, names of places are derived from churches. There is a Paternoster Row, an Amen Corner, and a whole district called St James's, as well as St Bartholomew's Hospital, St Pancras station, and so on.

Any overview of the Church of England must, therefore, take into account its historical and geographical context. To talk today of a church divided between the churchgoers and the non-churchgoers, is to ignore the way the Church of England is woven into the fabric of society. On any one Sunday there may be only a few people worshipping, but that congregation is *not* the Church of England. The Church of England is much wider than this; it consists of the millions of people who feel an attachment to the national church, who turn to it in times of need, and who describe themselves, when asked for their religion on hospital forms and the like, as C. of E. The church is not only those on the parochial church councils or the electoral rolls, it is everyone living in England who feels part of the spiritual heritage of the land and who has not opted for any other church or denomination. Their sense of history and geography is determined by the church to a greater or lesser degree, whether or not they profess any Christianity.

2
'And Also with You'

In 1980, when the Alternative Service Book (ASB) was published, its preface contained these words: 'The ASB, as its name implies, is intended to supplement the Book of Common Prayer not to supersede it.' A little later in the same preface, the authors wrote:

> Christians are formed by the way in which they pray, and the way they choose to pray expresses what they are. Hence those who seek to know the mind of the Church of England in the last quarter of the twentieth century will find it in this book.

Whatever the intention of the authors of the ASB, the survey carried out for this book undoubtedly shows that the Book of Common Prayer, which has been at the heart of Anglican worship for over three centuries, has now generally been nudged to one side. There has been a slow but thorough liturgical revolution.

It is easy to criticize the ASB on literary grounds, saying that it lacks the poetry of the old. The response 'And also with you' made by the congregation to the words 'The Lord be with you' sounds so ugly compared with the ancient alternative 'And with thy spirit', although, I must admit, when I was a child, I completely misunderstood what was meant by the Prayer Book response. Gradually, the Lord's Prayer has undoubtedly lost its rhythm, especially in the last paragraph of the modernized version, which reads, 'for the kingdom, the power and the glory are yours now and for-ever.' Many times, when regular churchgoers meet occasional churchgoers, the saying of the Lord's Prayer results in undignified confusion as the words 'Our Father who art in heaven' clash with 'Our father in Heaven' and the older conclusion to the prayer, 'for thine is the kingdom, the power, and the glory, for ever and ever. Amen', collides with the new.

All clergy were asked the question, 'On average each Sunday, how many services of Holy Communion do you celebrate according to (1) ASB Rite A, (2) ASB Rite B, (3) Book of Common Prayer?' Of all the celebrations of Holy Communion, 50 per cent used ASB Rite A, the version that uses the modernized language, and 12 per cent used Rite B, which retains the old language, but includes the opportunity to include the other liturgical changes, such as the exchange of a sign of peace. A total of 27 per cent of Holy Communion services were celebrated according to the Book of Common Prayer. What the survey was not able to show was what proportion of churchgoers attended which services, although I received the impression from other comments that the Book of Common Prayer was not used for the *main* Communion service but retained for other services attended by surviving traditionalists.

When it comes to baptisms the Book of Common Prayer is used in only 2 per cent of cases. Well over 80 per cent of parishes use the Alternative Service Book, with a number using local variations. When it comes to funerals, the Book of Common Prayer is still used in 11 per cent of cases, but over 60 per cent of funerals are conducted using the Alternative Service book and the remainder according to local variations, including, according to one respondent, the local crematorium's book. For weddings, 72 per cent are conducted using the ASB, with only 7 per cent using the Book of Common Prayer—and the remainder using an amalgam of the two. It is interesting to note the different reactions to the question on this point. The vicar of an urban parish in Cleveland noted that, when couples were given the choice, 40 per cent preferred the Book of Common Prayer. The vicar of a rural parish in Devon, however, a strong supporter of the idea that liturgical language should match contemporary language, said that, during preparation, couples were given the option, but, after studying the ASB, 'laughed the Book of Common Prayer out of court!' Another rural incumbent, this time from Cumbria, said that couples were given the choice and half opted for the old and half opted for the new. What did not come through from the survey, as the information was not sought here, was whether the couples who preferred the old service tended to be those who attended church less often.

While the twentieth century has been one of enormous secular change, at least the church has appeared to be changeless for much of the time; a symbol of the eternal and constant.

On the human level, today more people live to be a hundred years old than ever before. In the lifetimes of those celebrating their century in the 1990s, greater changes have taken place in society and to the environment than during any comparable period in human history. Today's centenarians will have witnessed the rise of the motor vehicle, the popularization of the telephone, the invention and increasing sophistication of the television, the availability of the radio, the arrival of the nuclear age, the building of motorways, the destruction of many towns, as well as immense social upheaval. During all this time, the church bore witness to matters eternal and it was assumed that it, too, would change little with time and fashions. Indeed, in the 1960s and 1970s, if visitors from the past, say one hundred years previously, could have found themselves in a church on a Sunday, they would have been able to recognize and understand most of what was going on. Admittedly changes took place in the nineteenth century that were far-reaching. The early Victorians would have endured two-hour services on a Sunday morning, starting with morning prayer, continuing with the litany and the first part of the Communion service, and ending with the sermon. Many churches during that time adopted High Church patterns of worship and, gradually, over the century, the morning service was shortened, with matins taking precedence. By the beginning of this century, and right up until the liturgical changes of the late 1970s and early 1980s, the standard pattern of worship on a Sunday in a church in England had developed a settled pattern of an 8.00AM Holy Communion service, an 11AM matins and a 6.30PM evensong. There would have been music and a sermon at both matins and evensong. Today, however, the pattern is very different. A 10 or 10.30AM morning service, usually centring on the Eucharist, is the main service each Sunday, any additional services being peripheral and expected to be poorly attended, catering for minorities. Often, too, baptisms are included in this morning service, whereas, in the past, baptisms were usually conducted as a discreet family occasion. The survey showed that 58 per cent of baptisms normally take place in the course of the main Sunday act of worship.

Let us look more closely at the subject of baptism as an example of what has happened. It is interesting to note that there is a growing tendency, not only to expect baptism to be part of *public* commitment, but also for it to take place after a period of preparation for the parents. Of clergy surveyed, 63 per cent said that the children of non-churchgoers would only be baptized after suitable preparation. One clergyman, who described himself as Evangelical and serves a rural parish, was typical in saying that, before baptizing a child, he would strongly encourage the parents to attend church if they were not already doing so. Similarly, the rector of a parish in Surrey, who calls himself a 'liberal Catholic', talked of trying to encourage attendance at church on the part of the parents while the details were being discussed. The rector of two rural parishes in Hertfordshire pointed out the difference between saying 'no' to a request made by a non-churchgoer for the baptism of a child and saying 'yes, if . . .'. The vicar of a suburban Lancashire parish, who was also an area dean, and a 'liberal' from a rural parish said that they welcomed children of all local residents to baptism, but an 'Evangelical' with a large rural town in his care in the Midlands had set up a local rule that he expected parents to attend church four times in a row before a child was baptized. A member of a team ministry covering a population area of 37 000 people, pointed out that church law says that he *cannot* refuse to baptize a child, but he liked 'there to be some attendance before the event.'

In the Alternative Service Book it is laid down that 'Holy Baptism is normally administered by the parish priest in the course of public worship on Sunday, but it may be administered at other times.' This is broadly similar to the instructions contained in the preamble to the public baptism section of the Book of Common Prayer, although it is my impression that public baptism was not normal practice in the recent past. For instance, while the funerals and weddings of members of the royal family have always been great public occasions, the head of the Church of England has never encouraged any of her family to give a boost to the idea or an example of public baptism when their own children have come to be named and admitted to the church.

The approach to baptism is one indicator of the tendency of the Church of England towards becoming less all-inclusive. It is certainly not the case today that all children are automatically baptized with no questions asked. The Christian commitment required in the baptismal vows are no longer tied up in ancient language. Parents and godparents are asked very directly if they are willing to give help and encouragement to the child by example and to ensure that he or she grows up to learn to be faithful in public worship and private prayer and to live by trust in God. They are also asked 'do you turn to Christ?' and are expected to answer 'I turn to Christ.' They are asked 'do you believe and trust in God the father who made the world, in his son Jesus Christ, who redeemed mankind, and in his

Holy Spirit who gives life to the people of God?' They are expected to reply firmly in each case, 'I believe and trust in him.' In the majority of cases these declarations of faith will be made in front of a congregation.

The Book of Common Prayer's private baptism of infants service, by contrast, includes the following question, full of ancient drama:

> Dost thou, in the name of this child, renounce the Devil and all his works, the vain pomp and glory of this world, with all covetous desires of the same, and the carnal desires of the flesh, so that thou wilt not follow nor be led by them?

It would appear that in former times godparents made the vows for the *child* and did not necessarily have to renounce these vices themselves!

These days, then, for someone unused to going to church, who knows few people in the congregation, to bring a child for public baptism or to agree to be a godparent is a daunting prospect. That the clergy require their attendance at church is another disincentive. Thus, for the nominal churchgoer to simply go to church for their child to be 'christened' as part of a folk-faith naming ceremony or first rite, has become increasingly difficult. However, it is not possible to draw the conclusion from this that church disincentives are directly responsible for the overall reduction in Anglican baptisms from 65 per cent of live births in 1900 to a current rate of under 30 per cent. It is a chicken and egg argument, for, as Robin Gill points out in his book *The Myth of the Empty Church*, 'baptisms were already in sharp decline before more restricted baptism policies were adopted by some parishes.'

So, while the 'unchurched' are losing touch with their spiritual heritage at parish level, it could be the case that this is happening at the national level, too. National avowals of unity have traditionally taken place within a Christian context, but today the opportunities for this are fading. No doubt a great State funeral for a much-loved member of the royal family would rekindle this sense of national fellowship and mystique, but even such an event would have but a temporary effect. This is because the number of British people who profess other faiths is growing and, further, there are few members of the royal family who are held in deep affection by the people at large.

Forty years ago, however, this was very different. Almost the entire population was glued to the small black and white television sets that showed the Queen being crowned in Westminster Abbey. This was a ceremony at the heart of a Christian nation. It was a solemn ceremony in which the Queen was declaring and invoking her divine right to rule. It was the Government and Establishment taking their cue from her to declare that God played an integral part in the workings of the British nation. As the Archbishop crowned the Queen, she was flanked by two other bishops, most memorably the then Bishop of Durham, later Archbishop of Canterbury, Michael Ramsey. The service included a ceremony that the television cameras were not permitted to intrude upon, that of the anointing of the new Queen with holy oil. It was mysterious and the mystique was deliberate. Over twenty-five years later, people watched the fairy-tale wedding in St Paul's Cathedral of the Prince and Princess of Wales. Here, too, the church gave its blessing to a match that was of importance to the couple *and* to the nation. However, much has happened since both these events took place. The remoteness of the royal family, the disintegration of the Prince and Princess of Wales' marriage, all have contributed to our sense of distance from the mystique at the heart of the constitution.

At the local level, a different kind of mystique has been lost from almost every parish in the land. A sense of timelessness has gone. The liturgy is in a new form, one that not only updated the language, but introduced a whole new concept to congregational life. No longer was the place of worship somewhere to be visited by an individual to meet a set of individual spiritual needs; the congregation, the worshipping family, is now all important. The new liturgy did not just update words, but changed the order and practice of worship. No longer is matins the normal morning service, but, instead, family Communion. This Communion, according to the Alternative Service Book, emphasizes the concept of the worshipping community. At one stage of the service it requires people to turn to their neighbours and shake their hands and give them a sign of peace. Occasional communicants find this embarrassing and difficult. British people like to keep a reserve in their relationships, like to keep a sense of personal space. To shake hands with or even embrace one's neighbour makes them uncomfortable. On the other hand, in so many churches around the country, there are the enthusiasts who wander around the church at this point, shaking as many hands and embracing as many people as possible.

It is a curious feeling to go into a new church and experience the sign of peace. Frequently, one senses that it is a divisive time, when those who are 'in' demonstrate this fact and those who are 'out', or occasional worshippers, sense isolation from the main group. Gavin Stamp, who was one of the contributors to the book *The Church in Crisis* in 1986, writes:

> Instead of the Peace being expressed ritualistically by the clergy in front of the altar, it is now obligatory for members of the congregation to 'share with one another a sign of Peace', that is, at least to shake hands with everyone within range. Many Anglicans indulge in this gesture with ruthless enthusiasm, even though few Englishmen normally shake hands as a conventional gesture of affection. Many Anglicans find all this acutely embarrassing; on the other hand, they are anxious not to appear as stand-offish so join in, but the Peace can, in fact, introduce tension and undermine that concentration on spiritual matters which it is surely the purpose of corporate worship to encourage in the individual.

Stamp continues:

> However the individual is now seen, not as a single soul seeking his own salvation, but as a member of the 'community' who is required to indulge in communal activities as well as acts of worship. This explains the growing importance of taking refreshments—usually coffee—after the service, a rite which often requires the construction of a coffee area with sinks and, inevitably toilets, within the church—facilities without which many Anglican churches have managed to survive for centuries.

Earlier in the book, Stamp had talked about the 'obsession with communities' in the new liturgies. In a deliberate attempt to return to the consciousness of the early church, the creed no longer begins 'I believe . . .' but 'we believe. . .'. However, for me, the most noticeable thing about the new liturgy is not the modernization of the language, although it has been stripped of much of its poetry, it is the reordering of the Communion service. There was certainly a case for providing an alternative set of words that would be more readily understood by a modern generation, but where was the justification in changing the order of the Communion service? The answer is that it was to reemphasize the concept of the worshipping community. In this context, the worshipping community means those who gather together in the church. The term 'Christian community', however, surely applies not only to them but to everybody else within the geographic area that is called the parish who is nominally or occasionally or even vaguely an adherent of the Christian traditions of these islands. These very people, though, are excluded by the new form of worship.

The survey revealed over and over again that substantial numbers of the clergy backed this exclusive approach. Of the clergy polled, 71 per cent prefer the new language and the new rite. Only 6 per cent state a preference for the Book of Common Prayer. They talk of their preference for the

liturgical order, of how people find the new words mean-
ingful, and how it brings the Anglican Communion service
more into the mainstream of the Western tradition of theological thinking. One respondent did say that he liked the
1662 Book of Common Prayer as a meditation and the Alternative Service Book sung with hymns as a joyful celebration. Those opting for Rite B—liked a new form, which
retained much of the old language—some respondents
talked about the modernity of the Alternative Service Book
with great enthusiasm, one saying that 'Jesus Christ was
born into 1993 as well as 1663 or AD 4 .' Even those who
prefer the Book of Common Prayer say rather meekly that
they like it because they are accustomed to it or that they
acknowledge themselves to be traditionalists or too old to
change. Though one respondent did say positively that the
Book of Common Prayer was the best language for worship, a number pointed out that the new version is an attempt to go back to the early church and that it is the Book
of Common Prayer, in fact, that is the more modern upstart.
In the early days, the Christians were not living in a Christian society—the folk-faith was paganism. They were the
exclusive minority. Attempts to revert to the feel of the early
church, therefore, imply that Christians are an exclusive and
chosen minority again within a sea of paganism. The ASB
can be seen, in this light, as being more in keeping with the
tradition, more understood by the people, more conducive
to a joyous celebration. No one says, though, as they do
with the Book of Common Prayer, that it has 'poetic reson-
ance'. Rather it is described as 'a book written by a
committee.'

Let us now hear some individual voices on this subject.
Sue Gunn worships at the small church of Rowborough
near Axbridge in Somerset. I met her during the filming of a
documentary programme shown last autumn called *The
Church of Two Englands*. She did not want to see the new
services being used in her church, though admitted that
they would have to come in the end:

I like the English of the old services. I don't like the modern English, the way it sounds, the way it comes off the tongue. The old English is better written than the new, but if there are people who like it then you must give it them, but I can't see why we can't have a bit of both because it's the older ones who do quite a bit of work in the church and if you upset a lot of them and they don't come to church, the church is going to lose out just as much as if you're not bringing the young ones in.

In the chapter on story and liturgy in *Believing in the Church*, the work of the doctrine commission of the Church of England published in 1981, John Barton and John Halliburton wrote the following:

One feature which is immediately striking to outside observers of Anglican worship is the continuing attachment to the divine office, whether in the form of cathedral evensong or Sunday matins in the parish church, and a tendency on the part of many English lay people to prefer the office to the Eucharist as the normal week-by-week form of worship. Clerical reformers in every century have tried with more or less success to reverse this trend, but it is only very recently that communicating attendance at the Eucharist has become the usual form of weekly worship for a majority of Anglican worshippers; and a preference for matins and/or evensong is still widely observable in many places. It is usual for theologians to be enthusiastic about the increasing tendency to accept the Eucharist as the normal Sunday service. But even if this is justified, it is important not to present the issue in such a way as to suggest that those who are committed to, say, sung matins are to be regarded merely as devotees of a 'bare' preaching service or a merely aesthetic exercise, whose purpose has nothing to do with that participation in, and appropriation of, the mysteries of salvation which is generally felt to characterize the Eucharist.

The authors go on to say that, whatever the historical origins of these elements of public worship:

> There can be no doubt that such means of recital of the Christian story are perceived by very many Anglicans to be themselves a form of prayer fully as important as Eucharistic worship in the liturgical life of the Christian community.

Another conclusion that could be drawn from these observations of twelve years ago is that many churchgoers at that time and before wanted to go to church, to experience the prayerful traditions of a sacred place and to re-enact certain familiar rituals, without wanting to commit themselves to an act of Christian worship. One can go to choral evensong in a cathedral or even to matins in a quiet parish country church and experience spiritual regeneration from the pattern of the words, the sound of the music, and the very history of the stones around. It is an individual experience and does not require, as does the Eucharist, a public exhibition of commitment. One sits in one's place and absorbs the real presence of God without having to come forward and take Communion or be badgered by one's neighbour to shake their hand. The introduction of the parish Eucharist as the main service of the week is all part of the trend away from individuals seeking a spiritual experience in their own way to requiring of them a public Christian commitment. The more that such requirements are made, the less likely are these people to come to church even though they are seeking a spiritual experience. These people are, therefore, left on the outside to join the 'unchurched'; the church begins to lose contact with people who have genuine spiritual needs.

Not long before my questionnaire landed on the doorsteps of a sample of parish clergy, another one had arrived, sent out by Doctor Robin Rees who wished to explore the state of music in liturgy. Doctor Rees published his survey in a book entitled *Weary and Ill at Ease*. He was able to demonstrate that, while some music is of a high standard and it greatly enhances worship, sometimes the music is so obviously of a low standard that it actually detracts from it and it is held back by incompetent musicians. In other cases, it appeared that good musicians were inhibited by clergy who were unable to appreciate or unwilling to allow music to play too full a part in worship. After all, music is directly accessible to the 'unchurched' and the spiritual responses it engenders are not expressed in words and cannot be kept within a tight dogmatic structure.

Doctor Rees concluded that:

> perhaps the most depressing finding of my survey was that there appeared to be little common ground between clergy and musical directors. The clergy had little knowledge of, or ability in, music while the directors' knowledge of theology was very limited. Moreover, there seemed little desire to develop this common ground.

The most familiar form of church music in England is the hymn, and an examination of favourite hymns produces some interesting observations. The favourite hymn of the nation, as identified by researchers from the BBC's *Songs of Praise* programme is 'Dear Lord and Father of mankind'. It ousted 'Jerusalem' from first place. It was favourite when a similar survey was conducted in 1985.

The rest of the top ten announced in 1993 was:

2 'The day thou gavest, Lord, is ended'
3 'The old rugged cross'
4 'How great thou art'
5 'Abide with me'
6 'Shine, Jesus, Shine'
7 'Make me a channel of your peace'
8 'The Lord's my shepherd'
9 'Love divine'
10 'Great is thy faithfulness'.

Members of St Mary's parish, Reigate, polled 240 people in the street and their results included many of the same hymns but a few additional ones. Their list was as follows:

1 'Jerusalem'
2 'All things bright and beautiful'
3 'Abide with me'
4 'The Lord's my shepherd'
5 'O Jesus I have promised'
6 'Onward Christian soldiers'
7 'Dear Lord and father of mankind'
8 'The old rugged cross'
9 'Shine, Jesus, shine'
10 'Morning has broken'.

The clergy I polled produced the following result:

1 'Servant king' (chosen by 11 per cent of clergy polled)
2 'My song is love unknown'
=2 'Thine be the glory'
=2 'When I survey the wondrous cross'
5 'O thou who camest from above'
6 'Love divine'
7 'And can it be'
=7 'Shine, Jesus, shine'
9 'Come down o love divine'
=9 'All my hope on God is founded'.

Can any conclusions be drawn from these three top tens? The first two are the choices of a wider group of people, including a substantial number of irregular churchgoers, and the third the choice of the committed. 'Shine, Jesus, shine' is the only hymn to make an appearance in all three lists. That old favourite, 'The old rugged cross', did not get a look in with the clergy; neither did 'Dear Lord and Father of mankind', 'Abide with me', nor 'The Lord's my shepherd'. The clergy's favourite, 'Servant King', appears to have made no great impression on the laity.

Although I did not ask the following question of the clergy, a survey in the issue of the *Church of England Newspaper* published in January 1993 asked its readers, who are, presumably, mainly regular churchgoers, 'What are your *least* favourite hymns?' The result was the following:

1 'Lord of the dance'
2 'All things bright and beautiful'
3 'Jerusalem the golden'
4 'I vow to thee my country'
5 'Shine, Jesus, shine'
6 'There's a friend for little children above the black blue sky'
7 'Immortal, invisible'
8 'Make me a channel of your peace'
9 'The old rugged cross'
10 'These are the facts as we have received them'.

It might well be deduced from all this that there is certainly a gap between the committed Christians and the 'unchurched' followers of Christian folk-faith when it comes to the choice of hymns—so much so that only *one* hymn bridges the gap and two hymns, 'The old Rugged cross' and 'All things bright and beautiful', are favourites with the nation but positively despised by the churchgoers.

It is difficult to tell from this evidence alone if a similar gap existed in times gone by. The popular hymn is a relatively new expression of worship and many of the favourites date only from the Victorian era. A glance at the various surveys suggests that the clergy are familiar with and like a higher proportion of modern hymns than the population at large. Certainly when it comes to liturgy, they express preferences for modern forms and modern prayers. It may be that, in recent times, the 'churched' have experienced a period of change and innovation, but that the 'unchurched' have not kept up with that change and, as a result, increasing numbers of the 'unchurched' find modern Anglican practices strange, even alienating.

3
'I'm the Vicar, Call Me Tim'

It was a cliché of the old repertory company farce that, at the moment of greatest embarrassment, when the maximum number of characters in the play had teamed up with the wrong partners or had their trousers down, the vicar would call. Today, however, the joke no longer applies—the vicar seldom calls, if ever.

It is one of the saddest symptoms of the increasingly inward-looking nature of the Church of England that, too often, the vicar is not seen out and about in the community as once he was and does not make it his business to call on everyone in a parish, whatever their denomination. For most of the modern generation, anyone calling at the door to introduce God is inevitably a Jehovah's Witness or a Mormon; the vicar does not get a look in. The statistics from the survey show this very clearly.

All clergy contacted were asked how many parishioners they had visited the previous week at home or in hospital and the answers ranged from none to 200. This latter figure was exceptional, due to preparation being made for a mission in an inner city parish with a civil population of 10 000 and an average Sunday attendance of 78. Overall, the average number of parishioners visited in a week was eleven and, of these, on average, six or seven of them were described as regular churchgoers . If, as it would seem from these figures, the average clergyman in England visits four members of the 'unchurched' population of his parish every week, and as some of these undoubtedly are visited in hospital or called on because of reports of ill health, or being visited for some specific purpose, perhaps to arrange a wedding or funeral, it can be implied that very little time is spent on 'cold calling'.

A rector from a rural parish with a civil population of just over 2000 and an electoral roll of 80 had visited just 1 parishioner the week before, but he did point out that he had also attended '8 meetings and committees'. In his parish magazine, at the bottom of the page giving the basic information about the parish, the words 'when sick please inform the rector' were written in capital letters.

In the past, it was a very important part of the vicar being the representative of the church for all that he was seen to call. He seldom took the opportunity of a call to Bible thump, but, often, an older person found it of comfort that the vicar came and perhaps said a short prayer at the end of the visit. The more affluent houses might have felt that they were obliged to provide some money for the church, but few objected. In former times the vicar also kept tabs on social need and could direct any local charitable giving or harvest produce to the families he felt were most in need.

I remember, as a youngster growing up in Devon in a parish where my father was the vicar, that I often accompanied him as he went around the small town where we lived delivering birthday cards. This was his way of keeping contact with the irregular as well as the regular churchgoers. Any child he christened received a birthday card for the first five years. If a family was large, he was a regular visitor at birthday times for many years. He stayed in the parish for over twenty years, and, eventually, was baptizing the children of those he had baptized as babies. Gangly adolescents and spotty louts in the street would recognize him as the vicar and he would know them by their Christian names. The only other person in the town with the same rapport was a formidable school teacher, then retired, who, with a few sharp words, could separate an argument between two of her formal pupils, even though both of them would be much taller than her.

In many ways this memory is a picture of an age that is gone. However, it shows what was possible, that with a system as simple as delivering a birthday card, the vicar could keep in touch. Today's clergy are too busy. They have paperwork to see to, meetings to attend, and their own faithful group to nurture and sustain. I remember once talking to the vicar of a group of rural parishes on the borders of England and Wales. He said, sadly, that, after a busy week, he often realized that he had not called on a single parishioner apart from those he needed to see on immediate church business. His busy life consisted of such tasks as filling out forms for diocesan officials, looking up ancestors for American visitors in the church register, and seeing to the needs of his regular and committed flock.

Many clergy see the way forward as being in preparing the laity to perform those tasks they no longer have time to do—the ordinary tasks of visiting the sick and preparing people for baptism or weddings. Many lay people are very good at doing these, but the modern vicar, perhaps, does not fully appreciate that *he* is the person most of the 'unchurched' want and expect to see.

Perhaps too many clergy feel uncomfortable about making visits to people with whom they will not be expected to discuss religion. They are too committed as Christians themselves, too steeped in the faith, too keen about the Saviour to want to make small talk over cups of tea or meet the generalized needs of people wanting the comfort of a folkfaith. They want commitment, declarations of belief, attendances at Bible classes, for individuals to become regular communicants. Many feel it is not their role to nurture an untargeted spiritual longing. I am not suggesting that clergy should behave with the extreme indifference to their faith as I recall exhibited by one Church of Scotland minister in my acquaintance. After visiting an old lady in his parish and making difficult small talk over tea and cake, he was about to leave the house when he said, rather begrudgingly, 'I suppose you'll want me to be saying a prayer before I leave?'

If the vicar *does* call on an unsuspecting parishioner, what sort of person will he be? Will he be anything like the Panama-hatted, cotton-jacketed, unworldly wimp of the stage or television situation comedy? There are a few of these around, but *very* few. When it comes to dealing with members of the regular congregation, the worshipping clique, the modern vicar cultivates the image of good-chum-come-elder-brother. Overwhelmingly, as the survey demonstrated, today's vicar or rector is not addressed by his title or surname, he is called simply by his Christian name. The 'I'm the vicar, call me Tim', sense of familiarity only alters in High Church parishes where he is more likely to be called Father Tim. One clergyman noticed, though, that there was an age gap in this regard, that younger people and people his own age called him by his first name, while members of the older generation were more formal. Writing in their parish magazines, clergy have variously signed themselves: 'Love Alan', 'God bless you all', 'Your friend and vicar', 'Father Iain', 'God bless you, David', 'Christ is risen! He is risen indeed!', 'Yours in the service of the living Lord', 'Your parish priest', 'Yours very sincerely', 'Yours Bill', 'Yours sincerely in our Lord', 'God bless you all, your friend and vicar', 'Yours in Christ' and 'Your sincere vicar'.

The typical modern vicar, rector, or priest in charge of a parish is, like his predecessors, usually married. Of those who responded to the survey, 85 per cent are married, 10 per cent single, with the separated or divorced outnumbering the widows by 4 cases to 3. Of those who are married, 84 per cent of clergymen said their spouses share their faith. Only in two cases did a clergyman admit that his wife did *not* share his faith, although 14 per cent of those asked the question decided not to answer. The answer that a wife shared the clergyman's faith was qualified with comments such as, 'yes, to some extent', 'mildly, in her own way', 'yes, but in a very different way' and the traditional picture of the vicar's wife being the self-sacrificing soul-mate and help-mate was not entirely borne out. Only 68 per cent of clergy's wives are involved in parish work and a substantial number have their own careers and paid employment. The jobs they have, however, are overwhelmingly in the service and caring professions, and there are many doctors, thera-pists, nurses, but over 20 per cent of all clergy in England, it seems, are married to teachers. In a few cases a wife shares the paid ministry as a deacon, one couple saying that they have always worked together, having trained for the minis-try together, and how the wife now works as a parish dea-con on a stipend. Today's clergy do appear to choose their wives from a very narrow range of occupations. Only one wife was in business for herself, owning a fabric shop, and all the occupations are undisputedly middle-class. Also, this section inevitably has a male bias. Only two of the respond-ents (less than 1 per cent) were women in charge of parishes.

As for clergy children, how has Christian family life rub-bed off on them? Reputedly, clergy children are free thinkers who verge on the tearaway. It is thought that they grow up resenting the family devoting itself so wholeheart-edly to the church and to all the pressures of having to behave and set an example. What, though, are the facts for these children today?

It is still the case that clergy children living at home are expected to go to church at least once on a Sunday. They appear to be let off very lightly compared to their forebears, who, as children living in the vicarage of even thirty or forty years ago, would have been expected to attend church or Sunday school at least three times on a Sunday. Between them, all the clergy approached had 412 children that were aged over 15. Of these, 75 per cent shared their father's faith, according to their fathers. When asked if he had prayed with his children when they were younger on a regular basis, 41 per cent of the clergy declined to comment, but, of those who did, only 26 per cent said 'yes', with 33 per cent saying 'no'.

When it comes to children under fifteen it is still very much the pattern that each child is expected to go to church once every Sunday. For this age group, 56.4 per cent of parents said they prayed with their children on a regular basis. It is interesting to note this increase in family devotions in vicarages in England.

From the financial point of view, it is quite clear that no ordained ministers are in their job for the money, which explains why at least 50 per cent of the clergy's wives work. Older clergy are better off if they have been ordained late in life—a number said they had a pension from a previous profession—for example, and, of course, how adequate the stipend is depends on what the required outgoings are. 'The stipend was adequate when I was living in a modern vicarage', said one, 'but now that I live in a large, lovely eighteenth/nineteenth century house, the heating bills are crippling—£1600 a year. It causes me considerable financial difficulty.'

It is difficult to quantify anything as intangible as morale among the clergy. There have been times in the history of the church when the clergy have been seen to be low in status, lax in their duties and indifferent to the needs of their congregation. There have been times, too, when worldly considerations have been given far more importance than spiritual ones. At one time, being ordained was just an extra qualification that went with another job. For instance, for many centuries, to be a don at Oxford it was obligatory to be an ordained member of the Church of England. The question I put to the clergy I contacted to tease this matter out was simply, 'Have you ever regretted seeking ordination?' The answer came back that nearly 80 per cent had *not* regretted their decision, but 17 per cent had; a few clergy declined to answer the question. From this it can be deduced that four out of five clergy working in parishes do not regret having answered the call.

The reasons given for regretting ordination were of a number of kinds. Some feel that following their own vocation has been hard on the family. Others yearn for a 'normal' nine to five job or for the freedom to be themselves. Some are exhausted by having to work such long hours. A few talk about the isolation of their position: 'I am a stranger', said one clergyman, who currently admits to being tempted to leave the ministry; others talk about loving their parish work, but being irked by the bureaucracy and the synodical government. A few complain about their bishop and the lack of support from above, and some talk about the issue of the ordination of women.

There were some more unexpected, yet perceptive, comments, too. For example, 'No, I have never regretted being ordained, but I have wept a lot and often feel furious', or 'I like being a priest, but I am less keen on being a vicar.' There was at least one respondent who, when asked if he would ever like to leave parish ministry, said, 'I just have.'

One or two have harsh words for their fellow Christians, accusing them of 'bloodymindedness', and describing cases where the most overtly committed Christians have been vindictive on a personal level. One of the most sweeping condemnations in the statements of regret came in the form of the reply, 'because tradition, dogma and unrealistic expectations make the job impossible.'

On the question of their personal faith, today's clergy are the usual Church of England mix of Evangelical, Anglo-Catholic and liberal; few describe themselves as 'chameleons', although one did. Some have flirted with Orthodoxy and one described himself as 'sinful (with Evangelical leanings).' When asked to describe themselves in church terms, the replies range from standard labels to some more detailed descriptions: 'Vatican to Anglican-Catholic with a smidgen of charisma', 'moderate Catholic/charismatic with growing Evangelical tendencies!', 'I hate labels but I am a sacramentalist.' One respondent did say when asked to categorize himself, 'I wouldn't !!! A plague on all your houses!'

Self-labelling can be a useful guide, but I asked two further questions to give me a fuller picture. I asked, 'Do you make a regular confession on a personal basis to a fellow priest?', and 25 per cent of the clergy said 'yes'. A few had made confession and do it irregularly, while a solid 70 per cent do not see it as part of their spiritual obligation. When asked, 'Have you ever prayed or spoken in tongues?', 28 per cent of clergy said 'yes', 68 per cent said 'no' and 4 per cent refused to answer. One clergyman said that he had tried, but it had never happened, another said he was not sure but possibly he had.

Speaking in tongues, or, glossolalia is the making of a sound that resembles language during a state of religious enthusiasm. Sounds come out without any conscious control and it is a form of religious expression that was common in the early church. The biblical precedence for it is to be found in the Book of Acts at the time of Pentecost and the continuing use of tongues was noted in 1 Corinthians by St Paul. Throughout most of the history of Christianity it has been very much a minority practice, concentrated mainly in and around certain congregations or sects, but undergoing periodic waves of revival. Evidence that such a high proportion of numbers of ordained clergy should now be experiencing the gift of tongues suggests that a similar revival movement is at work in certain parts of the Church of England at present. Many see the charismatic revival as bringing the church back in line with the early Christian movement. Certainly the liturgical changes that have been introduced have attempted to go back to the early days.

At a conference organized by Anglican renewal ministries in March 1993, the Reverend Michael Mitton, told 400 clergy and church leaders that the charismatic renewal was not a fringe activity, but one that is increasingly becoming part of the mainstream of church life. Another speaker at the conference in Swanwick in Derbyshire was Bishop Michael Marshall. He told those present that:

God was preparing his church for persecution and suffering. Crisis within the church would be beneficial if it brought it to its knees. . . . renewal comes to a church that knows its need for God.

In this he was expressing a common feeling that the current Church of England is a minority group that is holding fast to a truth within a pagan community. To the 'unchurched', however, speaking in tongues is likely to appear weird and bizarre, and the charismatic movement has thus only further distanced the 'churched' from the 'unchurched'.

The Church of England could be said to be gradually remodelling itself in certain respects on the notion certain activists have of the pre-Roman, pre-Biblical model, when the church was not in any way associated with the State or established religion, but, rather, was a minority faith under persecution. This is certainly the way many clergy appear to see themselves at the moment—as members of a minority faith at odds with the world. It needs to be remembered, of course, that the early Christians were very much involved in a messianic movement, a movement that believed that the return of the Messiah and the culmination of the purpose of God on earth was going to happen soon. Similarly, today, as the year 2000 is approached, an exaggerated belief that the end is nigh is to be found in a number of movements. It is associated with the end of the millennium, and the church today, as it was in the late AD 900s, is not immune to millennia fever.

The section on speaking in tongues in the survey produced perhaps one of the most significant of all the findings of the survey. Fifty years ago (although I know of no equivalent survey in which the question was asked in this way), it would have been very surprising to have found even 5 per cent of clergy admitting to having prayed or spoken in tongues. At the beginnings of the current charismatic revival, speaking in tongues was very much a suspect, fringe activity, best left to the Pentecostal movement. Today, nearly 30 per cent of clergy, including bishops, and probably the Archbishop of Canterbury himself, have had a charismatic experience. In some churches, some have feared that in some way one is not a true Christian, or is not giving oneself over to Jesus sufficiently, if one has not received the gift of tongues. Charismatic congregations tend to be some of the very strongest, expanding groups in the church, and yet, also, the most dogmatic. There is little room in the truly 'born again' church for the spiritual dabblers and those who just want reassurance in an English folk-faith kind of way. One has to be committed to join the Christian party. So, the high numbers of clergy active in the charismatic movement could be interpreted as another sign that the church is becoming more exclusive, more of a denomination, and less open to the nation as a whole.

One set of answers that the Roman Catholic church might find useful to consider, accompanied the following question: 'To whom would you normally turn for personal or spiritual advice?' Overwhelmingly, clergymen responded that their wives are their greatest support. Sometimes a close friend or family member or even a fellow member of the clergy was also of help, but, when it came to asking about the pastoral role of the archdeacon or the bishop, replies were less favourable. Some were even quite scathing, their comments ranging from, 'even the bishop on occasion!' to 'our present suffragan is so pastoral, that this is almost the only time in my ministry that my bishop has been approachable and caring!', 'I find many people don't really listen', 'it has been my great sadness that during the past six months of quite serious illness I haven't seen the diocesan bishop; the suffragan bishop visited me once in hospital. I haven't seen the archdeacon at all. In the local diocese one asks who cares for the carers?'

One clergyman said that a member of his congregation had wisdom and common sense that he greatly appreciated and another said that, when needing guidance, he just looked for a sign from God. Another said that he consults whoever he feels led to confide in, 'but it is unlikely that it would be a member of the modern hierarchy.'

It is worth noting that, relatively speaking, the archdeacon is not highly valued as a counsellor, contact with the bishop being made more often instead.

Today's clergy are far from being the homogeneous group they might have once been. A century ago, it was traditional for the younger sons of the middle and upper classes to seek ordination as an alternative to going into the Army as they were not going to inherit the family estates. Once ordained, these younger sons were given the family living where they might have stayed for most of their lives. Today, legally and structurally, the church parish system is very different from what it once was. There is a centralized selection procedure and appointments are made at both national and diocesan levels. Frequently, the clergy are members of team ministries and do not have the traditional parish freehold that they once had. There is retirement which in the old days was unusual. In the past, once the parson was appointed, he could stay for life, enjoying all of the legal perks of the freeholder. He could do pretty much what he liked with his church and even allow the congregation to dwindle away. It was certainly not unknown for the appointee to be an absentee. The term 'vicar' itself, now popular as the term for the incumbent, was like 'curate'—a word to imply that a representative of the true freeholder, that is the rector, was present in the village to conduct the necessary services.

Today, the survey revealed that 58 per cent of the current clergy in Britain have professional or vocational qualifications other than those they have acquired in order to be ordained. There are dentists, geologists, civil engineers, retired civil servants, Army officers, local government administrators, bankers, accountants, solicitors, geography teachers, computer engineers, musicians, youth workers, forestry workers, telecommunication experts, and many others who have sought ordination *after* pursuing another career. The career ordinand, who leaves university and goes direct to theological college, is not now the norm.

In terms of interests, both intellectual and other, there seems to be little homogeneity. All respondents were asked which three books they had read in the last three years that had most influenced them. Only twenty-five clergy selected the Bible in reply, and they were, in the main, in the Evangelical camp. However, it would be unfair to draw the conclusion that less than 10 per cent of clergy had been influenced by the Bible in the last three years. I suspect that, like interviewees on *Desert Island Discs* when asked by Sue Lawley which book they would take with them as castaways, they are allowed to assume that the Bible and Shakespeare are taken for granted. The Bible was included, however, in the most extraordinary short list of three chosen by one respondent. It was joined by *Billy Bunter* and the *Oxford Book of Death*, although I am not sure how seriously his answers should be taken. Of the other replies which appeared particularly note-worthy, the rather sad, 'I am not a great reader, regrettably' needs to be reported along with 'none in particular (except the Bible!)' Of the less expected books to appear in a survey of clergy reading *The Leadership Secrets of Attila the Hun*, must, presumably, have served some purpose, perhaps giving guidance as to how to chair a parochial church council!

One author, however, appeared in more lists than any others, being read by nearly 10 per cent of the sample: Gerard Hughes, with his book *God of Surprises* being the one most commonly selected. Second place went to books by or about Bishop Michael Ramsey, followed by a long list of authors attracting the interest of between 2 per cent and 3 per cent of the clergy polled. These included in order of popularity, Bishop Richard Holloway, Matthew Fox, Sheila Cassidy, Bishop John Taylor, Bishop Lesslie Newbigin, John Stott and Susan Howatch. Among the also-rans were Archbishop George Carey, David Watson, Bishop David Jenkins, John

Wimber, Wesley Carr, Bishop Michael Marshall, Hans Küng, Martin Israel, Angela Tilby, and Stephen Hawking.

Only five clergy admitted to having bought no books at all in the previous year, although it was pointed out by a number of clergy that it was more cost-effective to go to the local library than to the local bookshop. The average number of books bought by the parish clergy in the survey, though, was ten each in the course of last year. One admitted to having bought sixty books and another twelve bought over thirty-five books in the twelve-month period, although it must be said that, in some cases, books were not being bought purely for private study, but in connection with teaching obligations.

When it comes to prayer, my survey asked how much time each member of the clergy spent in private prayer a week. Bearing in mind that the daily office is a minimum requirement, it would appear that some clergy must gallop through it at an extraordinary rate. One admitted to just half an hour, another said 'very little', while others said they talk to God anywhere and a lot, some set up to fifteen hours aside for prayer. One talked about saying the daily offices and his practice of being constantly aware of the will of God. Others admitted that they prayed a 'rather pathetic' two or three hours a week, or said 'not enough time' or 'too little'. Another said he was praying all the time as he went about. An average, though, was around three hours a week, which is about the time it takes to say the daily office. In other words, the modern clergyman does the bare minimum of private praying, and, apart from Sunday services and official occasions, more time, I would suggest, is spent in parish administration than in prayer. In terms of private study, there was a wide range of responses. For many, private study is orientated towards preparing the sermon; others were quite honest and said 'very little' or 'not a lot', although one admitted to spending fifteen hours a week in study, but he was involved in researching for a postgraduate degree in New Testament studies. It would be difficult, then, to describe the average parish clergyman as a man of prayer and scholarship, although exceptions do exist. In this they probably vary little from their forebears. In the old days, however, this might have been interpreted as suggesting that many clergy were indifferent to their professed faith, but today, the fact that nearly 30 per cent speak in tongues, together with other evidence from the survey, suggests that this is unlikely to be the case.

Further research into this area might reveal that today private prayer is less important than communal prayer. Today's clergyman spends time in Bible study classes, small prayer groups and healing groups and in general religious fellowship—far more time, most probably, than in private prayer. He certainly takes fewer services in each church than he would have done once, and, indeed, many concentrate their efforts on the one Sunday morning act of worship. As we saw earlier, the evidence suggests that he is not out visiting. A picture of the modern clergyman produced by A. N. Wilson in *The Church in Crisis* has a certain ring of truth, to it.

When the laity speak of clerical idleness they are not always thinking of those rather amiable old-fashioned parsons who sat in their rectories doing nothing in particular. They are often thinking of the new breed of man who fills his day with bustle and meetings and paperwork, but who really gets very little done in the way of remembering 'the greatness of the trust . . . committed to your charge'. The type is familiar, he is addicted to copying machines, stencils and typewriters. It is impossible to attend the simplest liturgical function in his church without having a sheaf of such papers thrust into one's hand. Side by side with complicated explanations of the diocesan synod, or potted analyses of how the vicar would solve the unemployment problem, there are whimsical requests for jumble, baking or garments, whose invariable exclamation marks provide such an air of frenzy.

56

I am sure it was not a view of this kind that the Managing Director of the Christian Resources Exhibition, Gospatric Home, had in mind when he said that computers had finally come into their own in the church office and the vicar's study. At the 1993 exhibition, he proudly claimed there were more computers, printers and software available than ever before, and programs have been devised for compiling services, running parish magazines, and even mapping out graves in the churchyard. At the exhibition was a stand bearing the title 'Vestry 2000', which was a futuristic look at the way a parish office could use the latest technology. The exhibition which took place in May 1993 over a four-day period had 363 stands, and was visited by nearly 10 000 people. In the world of business, it is a well-known fact that the wonders of information technology have done nothing to save paperwork, indeed quite the opposite. When new computer programs are invented, their users find that tasks they previously thought of as unnecessary take on a new urgency. The same inevitable progress is at work in the church.

I have one friend, a non-stipendiary priest, who has another job and has charge of five rural parishes. I once asked him how he managed, given that so many clergy claim to be overworked. His answer was simple: 'I throw every piece of paper that comes my way into the wastepaper bin. If it's important they'll phone me.'

Could old-fashioned forms of parish outreach however be realistically revived? Could parish visiting be given a new boost? Today, there are many parishes in England where this should still be possible. Assuming a civil population of 4000 per ordained member of the clergy, that involves 1500 households, so a vicar would only need to visit 30 a week in order to make contact with every household in the course of a year. Talk to anyone who is involved in house-to-house calls, be they political canvassers or door-to-door salespeople, and they will say that thirty calls a week is easily done. Indeed, the survey found that one man had, exceptionally, visited 200 people in a week. Even if at every household the vicar had to stay to talk at any length, which is exceedingly unlikely, there would still be time left in the average week for private prayer, study and taking services. Perhaps only the paperwork would need to be set aside.

Such an approach, however, might require caution in some inner city parishes. The Reverend Duncan Ross at Hackney Wick in East London had the unpleasant experience of being mugged as he was calling at a flat in one high-rise block. His experience demonstrates how an inner city ministry presents some very different challenges to those of a rural one.

In Hackney Wick, just over a hundred years ago, benefactors from Eton College founded the church of St Mary of Eton. Even though the church is not that old compared to many, it is already beginning to aquire some of the attributes of a sacred place in the middle of an urban 'village'. Inside the church, it has a glorious, tall, airy feeling. It follows a High Church tradition, with accompanying smells and ritual. Outside, opposite the church, is a huge tower block, and, whereas in a rural village people look up to the church from their homes, in Hackney Wick, people can look down from the upper storeys of the tower block on to the church tower of St Mary of Eton.

When the church was first set up, there was dire poverty in the East End, but today the Reverend Duncan Ross says that poverty of a much subtler kind is to be found in the area:

There are people in my parish whose children perhaps have just one pair of shoes per year. I have come across families where they are unable to pay for school dinners, yet, next door to them, there would be people living who are far better off than I am, who have a car and a lot of material wealth and possessions. But what people have in common is some sort of inner poverty, poverty of worth, that you don't feel you mean very much or are worth very much if you live in an area like ours. This is a great shame because there are people of tremendous value and tremendous worth here, but they don't believe in themselves; it's a much subtler kind of poverty in that sense. If you live twenty storeys up in a tower block and no one wants to hear your problems and no one will answer the phone when you ring you begin to slowly feel that you are stranded and you don't count and it's that lack of self-worth that I think is common to our area.

What did the Reverend Duncan Ross see as the role of the church in this?

It's a very simple one. I think the church has to be a sign of what is possible, that people can actually be themselves and love one another, not in some backslapping sense, but in the sense of allowing one another to be themselves, and allowing one another to show their worth. It's no use believing you're worth something unless you can actually display it and someone else can value that or receive that. And I feel our task is very simple and very visible and being a community of Christians. I've observed through the eighties that this does work and people grow and stand up and believe they're worth something and are able to go to the places in which they work and reflect this to other people that they are worth something. It's very simple, very subtle and very invisible.

There is fear in the area and opposites live together very closely. That's a feature of where we are. Whether it's poverty compared to wealth or fear compared to hope. We, as the church, live with both of these; we live across the divide. I think that is part of our task. There *is* fear, but I have to say that some of the people who are fearful are also some of the most resilient who give me hope.

Very often the greatest spiritual riches are to be found among the 'have nots'. That's an easy thing to say, but it is purely based on my experience. Some of the most remarkable people that I've known inside and outside my congregation have been people who, in other terms, have had very little, seemingly very little in their lives materially or even emotionally, given to them. I have to say their faith in their spirituality has made them into greater people. These are the people I am very proud of.

The church must always be where the people are, and by that I don't mean the people who come to church, I mean where the people live.

To take another example, the Reverend Eileen Lake was brought up not far from St Mary's in Hackney Wick. She is now an Anglican deacon and a hospital chaplain. She sees the church playing a significant role in the lives of many people in the inner cities in pastoral terms.

In terms of helping them to get better services from the council, helping people with problems who can't cope or helping people at the local school. We're always running around and trying to write letters and see the right people and trying to get things done and improve their standard of living physically as well as emotionally.

In Hackney we're not talking about a poverty level where children are hungry, but they may be badly nourished, living on diets that are not varied, lacking the right nutrients, and vitamins, and so on. They live on a diet of fast foods that people don't have to take much time over.

What of the spiritual diet?

The spiritual diet is being all together, and suffering together, and holding each other up in that suffering. Knowing that you're all in the same boat, and that there is some hope, and that there is something to look forward to, something to aim towards. It's a difficult thing to explain to people when they're feeling very hopeless. All we can do as the church is just to be alongside them, hold their hand when they need a hand to hold, and just be with them, and weep with them if necessary. Sometimes you can't do anything else but weep. I can think of times when I've been with families where there's been domestic violence and the children are affected—not directly, but emotionally. They see that their mum is being beaten up by dad, or their dad is hardly ever home. Perhaps they don't even know where dad is.

There *is* violence in the area, but I'd like to say that there is less now than there used to be. I'm not sure why that is; I would like to think that is was something to do with the presence of the church in the area and getting to know people, trying to have some sort of community feel in the area. Standards of living have risen, but that is not to say that there aren't still places in which people are in direct poverty.

The old model of rural parish ministry involved the church being at the heart of a geographically defined parish and being available to all to meet spiritual and material needs. While the tendency today in the cities is for the churches to abandon this model, the example of Hackney Wick shows that it is still possible for the church to be at the heart of an 'unchurched' community and for the clergy to be there to meet the needs of the people. A modern urban parish is not like the rural parish of old, where the boundaries were defined by landscape features. It might simply consist of a set of high-rise blocks, a new estate, or the catchment area for a shopping centre. The problem is that, in many urban areas, the parish system appears to have fallen into disuse, with churches encouraging eclectic bands of worshippers. The survey showed overwhelmingly how it was that the churches which gathered congregations from the widest area were invariably the urban ones, while, in rural districts, people still tended to go to the parish church rather than seek out a specific worshipping community which met all their preferences. Eclectic congregations do not tend to welcome the occasional churchgoer, preferring *not* to meet the general needs of the 'unchurched', so, unless the parish system can find a means of revival in the urban areas, the gap between the 'churched' and the 'unchurched' will continue to widen in the places where most people live.

4

Forgive Us, Lord, for We Have Synod

At the heart of the Church of England's organizational structure is Church House, Westminster. It must rank as one of the most confusing buildings ever constructed. The only way to find one's way around is to adopt the tactics advocated in *Alice Through the Looking Glass*: always head away from where you want to go, and sooner or later, you will end up at your destination. The reason the building is so difficult is that it is built around, and designed to service, the great circular hall where the General Synod meets.

For most of the year, to be inside Church House is very much like being inside any one of the Government departments in neighbouring Whitehall: gentlemen in grey suits and mature, sensible secretaries pad along the corridors. However, for two weeks, the place hums with activity. Earnest members of the House of laity from the shires rub shoulders with archdeacons and rural deans, and bishops, in their purple fronts, are three a penny when the General Synod meets.

At these meetings, the number of members in the circular chamber will directly reflect how much interest there is in the subject being debated. Obscure measures, to do with, say, the size of gravestones, will attract just a few enthusiasts, but key debates, like that in the Autumn of 1992 on the ordination of women to the priesthood, result in the Synod chamber being crammed. The balcony, too, will reflect the wider interest or otherwise in the proceedings: there can be times when the gallery is crowded with public, press and broadcasters, and, under the glare of the television lights, it seems as if the whole nation is listening to the Synod. It was the Archbishop of Canterbury, for instance, who first broke the news to the nation of the engagement of the Prince and Princess of Wales while at a Synod meeting. All the news media had embargoed press information but the news could only be broadcast once the news was officially out.

A flow chart published in the Church of England Year Book shows the structure of the Synodical government of the Church of England. It looks much like a complicated diagram of an electrical circuit. Annual parochial church meetings send representatives to parochial church councils and deanery synods. The deanery synods consist of two groups: the clergy and the laity. The laity send representatives to the diocesan synods and also to the General Synod. The houses of clergy at the deanery level send their representatives on to diocesan level.

Parallel to this process, the archdeacons and clergy of the dioceses vote for representatives to sit on the convocations of Canterbury and York. Similarly, the deans and provosts send some of their number to the house of clergy, as do religious communities, and university and service chaplains. The diocesan bishops, in turn, sit in the houses of bishops of the convocations of Canterbury and York by virtue of their office, and a group of suffragan bishops are appointed to join them. The convocations then, as one entity, become the house of bishops and the house of clergy at the General Synod, and, when joined with the house of laity, form the final legislative body of the Church of England. The General Synod is, then, served by assorted committees, the most important being the Standing Committee. There is a legislative committee and various subcommittees of the Standing Committee, including the Standing Orders Committee. Then there are advisory committees and permanent commissions, and, under the General Synod office, are the Record Centre and the Enquiry Centre, plus other bodies with a variety of specific jobs.

Forgive Us, Lord, for We Have Synod

Before every General Synod meets, its members are sent the agenda. It is not a simple document. Indeed, it is so complicated that sections have to be coloured as well as numbered to enable members to find their way around. Only the experienced Synod hand can tell which items will appear at what time and what importance should be given to each. Legislation, measures and Canons are interwoven into the structure of the agenda alongside resolutions and reports from committees and commissions. The General Synod has never made up its mind as to whether it is a legislative body or a debating chamber.

Once every year, everything is transported up to York, a little like a royal progress, or the transportation of the European parliament around the community. The Synod holds its summer meeting at the campus of York University, where members stay in student rooms and walk across pleasant lawns, past duck ponds, to get to the main debating hall. When the weather is hot, it can take on something of the appearance of a holiday camp. It can be an informal occasion, with all members eating together, so a curate can find himself sitting next to his bishop, discussing the world over a boiled egg.

If the ordinary person in the pew, or even the occasional churchgoer derived their image of the church solely from the General Synod, it would be very misleading. Although it does take some important decisions that filter down to parish level, much of the time the Synod has the atmosphere of a gentleman's club. Parliament at Westminster has been described as the best club in London, but in deserving that title it must have been a close run competition with the General Synod. Indeed, there are a few individuals who have been members of both 'clubs' simultaneously and had to dash from one building to the other, from the House of Commons to Church House, as party whips and synod business managers dictated. Although, this clubby atmosphere has changed of late, no doubt, it will re-establish itself as new Synod members and the new paid office-holders become established.

Up until two years ago the tone was set by the genial bachelor Secretary-General, Derek Pattinson—later to become the Reverend Sir Derek on retirement. He presided over Synod briefings in formal, striped trousers and black coat with a glass of red wine in his hand. His successor, Philip Mawer, is a younger, thinner, sharper man, neatly suited and exuding management efficiency. Thus, in his way he is as indistinguishable from the Whitehall fast-track, first-division officials of today as Sir Derek was from the old school mandarins of his, for the church bureaucracy is modelled far more closely on a government department than it is on a religious community.

Dissatisfaction with this set-up emerged as a consistent theme in criticisms from the clergy. Over and over again in the survey it was the bureaucracy of the present organization that was described as a dead weight sinking the church. As to how this situation could be overcome, one of the more radical suggestions came from Merseyside. The suggestion was for the bishops to keep quiet and for the General Synod to be suspended for ten years. This respondent's concerns, if not his solution, were shared by a clergyman from Cheltenham: 'I am desperately worried about the future of the Church of England. The General Synod is too powerful.' Also, one Evangelical clergyman from rural Sussex called for, 'a cut back in bureaucracy at diocesan level', with a corresponding opportunity for more local freedom of worship. From Cumbria came this suggestion:

We need to invert the present tendency towards a centralized bureaucratic hierarchy that values the 'centre' as 'above' and see the pastoral unit as the cutting edge of our mission to the nation. Bishops should visit their clergy on a regular basis. If they are exercising a function on his behalf in the parishes, he ought to develop a personal ongoing link. Listen to this calculation: if two bishops had 300 clergy to cover between them, each would have 150. If they both manage their diaries to cover three periods of one hour each week, they could visit every one of their clergy once a year. If such a pattern seems too much, revise it to a mere three hours every fortnight. They should discuss with and meet their clergy on site.

A prayer-book Catholic from Yorkshire said, 'Nothing can replace the parochial system. Synodical government has lost, if it ever had it, the confidence of both clergy and people. Hopefully it will go.' Also, a 'liberal' from rural Cornwall expressed the view, 'I don't believe synodical government is working. The church should consider returning to rule by bishops alone.'

The clergy were asked to share their concerns about the Church of England and, repeatedly, matters of structure emerged. There was no general agreement, but what follows is a flavour of the opinions given and a possible set of structural reforms which I have put together drawing on ideas thrown up by the survey. A cross-section of clergy opinions first.

From a suburban/rural parish in Bath, came the view that, in any future reorganization, the Church of England should 'avoid management efficiency models. The church should maintain the parish ministry, even if more non-stipendiary ministers, especially in rural areas, are ordained.' He also said that there should be more buildings shared by the Church of England and other churches and denominations. A clergyman from Warwickshire detected:

> . . . too much emphasis on managerial methods! I wasn't ordained to define goals! Dioceses now seem to dictate to the parish priest what shall be done. Parishes meanwhile vote with their feet. My job is with people and I find that getting alongside them is rewarding, but time-consuming. Bishops, it seems, want success! Faithfulness to God does not necessarily count any more. Our privilege is to be established, our responsibility is to a total community. Present trends point to a desire for a

confessing church looking after its own and it can't do that properly without priests!

From rural Dorset came the view that the church should 'encourage locally ordained ministry, leave clergy free for prayer, inspiration, people in crisis who need direction. Free the church from administration and paperwork.' An incumbent from Maidenhead also regretted the tendency for clergy to become more administrators than pastors. The parish ministry got strong backing from two clergy with rural parishes, one in the Oxford diocese, the other in Staffordshire: 'There should be a concentration of funds and manpower on parish ministry', and 'I would like to see more control given to parishes.'

Another side of the argument was also put, generally voiced by those who saw the church as not being there for the 'unchurched'. An Evangelical from Congleton, who described himself as quietly charismatic, talked of 'a freeing of parish boundaries, which no one recognized except the clergy.' Also, an inner city liberal wrote:

> . . . Evangelical congregations are expanding. Church planting is on the increase in south London. What I think ought to happen is the development of a kind of twentieth-century urban monasticism. We need centres of community and excellence that are hospitable to the world and creative to the reinterpretation of the Gospel.

From Suffolk came talk of accepting a reduction in full-time ministers and proactively planning for this by amalgamating and closing parishes where necessary, and training men and women specifically for multiparish ministry. From Devon came the observation that, in the Exeter diocese:

> . . . we seem to have swung from a philosophy of the gradual process of only maintaining key settlement churches (no one actually admitted it) to keeping all churches open with a full-time ministry of 'enablers'

supervising several churches with local ministry fulfilling all that is necessary within each parish.

Although an Anglo-Catholic from an urban parish in North Shields was one of those who called for a rationalization of buildings, from suburban Halifax came a call for ending the parish system, as 'boundaries are meaningless to people and wasteful of clergy time and resources.'

Such clergy, calling for a slimming down of the Church of England in terms of buildings and stipendiary staff, would be heartened by news from a town parish in Somerset where the incumbent talked of detecting a small but significant change in the life of the church:

People are becoming more confident in their faith and more ready to share what, up until recently, had been a very private matter for them. One of my anxieties about the future is that the conservation lobby is making us prisoners in our buildings.

Agreement with this view, that buildings are holding back ministry came from an urban parish in Devon where the vicar said that years of keeping the system going at any cost was finally coming to an end:

Propping up buildings that are listed will no longer be possible. The ministry as I knew it when I was ordained in 1957 has changed because the world has changed; society has, and the church has, almost without some realizing it.

A suggestion that the parochial ministry should be phased out and the buildings be given priority, however, came from Bristol:

This change should take place over a reasonable period of time. Local, non-stipendiary ministers should replace the present clergy. This would release central church funds for our heritage of ancient buildings and remove some of the heavy financial burdens on our faithful lay supporters.

Such a line was totally contradicted by the incumbent of a suburban parish in Lincoln: 'We should stop maintaining empty churches in rural areas.' A liberal Catholic from Loughborough was also clearly on the side of those who felt that '. . . the burden of maintaining a church building will continue to distract parishes with ancient plant.'

Financial worries were the concern of an incumbent from a rural parish in Northumberland, who described himself as an evangelical charismatic. He said that the majority of his energy was spent raising funds and dealing with financial matters; 'I think that the Church of England will bankrupt itself.' This was also felt by a clergyman from suburban Cheshire: 'I fear we might be moving towards a financial crunch that will contribute to a further decline in the number of clergy.' Equally, the view of one suburban respondent from Birmingham was that pure economics will necessitate the closure of more churches: 'There will have to be a reduction in incumbencies and a greater concentration on team ministries.'

Certainly financial worries led the concerns of the clergy. Many find themselves spending inordinate amounts of time raising relatively small amounts of money to maintain an important part of their fabric. The trouble with raising money is that it requires administration and paperwork. No wonder so many feel financially frustrated.

When asked about the faculty system within the church, the survey came up with the following answers: 68 per cent thought that the regulations were acceptable, but 27 per cent believed them to be too strict; 1 per cent said they needed tightening and 4 per cent were either unsure or declined to answer.

Preserving old buildings is not a priority favoured by one priest from rural Gloucestershire. He believes that the church will have to close some of its ancient structures because of 'the attitude of English heritage, which considers very "old" buildings a museum and not the live heart of the community.'

Forgive Us, Lord, for We Have Synod

Raising money at parish level through the quota system, whereby each worshipping congregation is given a target of money it is expected to raise for the diocese according to the size of its electoral roll, is a matter that raises grumbles, but also general agreement that it is probably the best system available. The survey asked clergy if the quota system appeared to them to be fair, and the results were as follows. Almost 80 per cent believe the system to be fair, 15 per cent said it is not, and an extra comment from suburban Derby was that 'the system is going to implode within a few years and good riddance!'

From a rural town in Kent came the following view from a 'radical Evangelical' on the subject of parish ministry, one of the greatest financial costs to the church:

> I believe our church needs to aim realistically to have a priest for every parish church. My own experience shows how a church is crippled by having to share a minister . . . Sadly our church seems to be heading in the opposite direction. At parish level, clergy must give lay people more responsibility.

This view was backed up by a prayer-book Anglican from Shropshire who was concerned about the way the church was going: 'Rural life, which concerns me, is likely to be affected by further reduction of clergy to the detriment of the church.' Interestingly, a clergyman from an urban parish in Birmingham showed a similar concern for the predicament of rural parishes, forecasting that more parishes will be amalgamated to united benefices in rural areas, and suggested a solution:

> It would be better if a locally ordained person, permanently resident in a parish, could ensure that each church has at least one service on Sunday, without the incumbent having to dash around.

Yet this idea was countered by a vicar from an urban London parish, whose argument was that there should *not* be a priest for every parish.

There are too many priests working on their own. Too many large buildings, difficult to maintain. The church needs to train its clergy for collaborative ministry, seeking to use their gifts, teaching them to use the gifts of the laity.

However, he did support the idea of asking clergy over sixty or sixty-five to spend five to ten years or more looking after a country church in a small village, which might be a better idea than buying a retirement home on the south coast.

Other clergy talked of retaining parishes and treating them as the most important units. One such, from Norfolk, added that there should be an insistence that 'bishops must have at least ten years' experience in parochial ministry, preferably more and in at least two types of parish!' 'Reinforce and build up parish ministry', was the message of a respondent from the Liverpool diocese who was critical of the centralization that he said was developing in his area.

Linked to this, an impatience with the old ways and assumptions came through in the comments from a charismatic Evangelical ministering in a suburban/rural parish in Essex. He saw the real growth as being in the charismatic parishes and was quite willing to see the parish boundaries, which he described as formerly thought of as sacrosanct, being crossed more and more as 'we follow the Holy Spirit's leading. I see ahead large parishes investing in growth rather than propping up dead wood.'

If, however, investing in larger parishes involves the creation of more team ministries, one respondent from a rural town in Hertfordshire would not be impressed: 'We have experienced an experimental group ministry of fourteen parishes; it has not worked.' A charismatic Evangelical from Lancaster also called for the end to team ministries which '. . . dilute flair and create monochrome superparishes.'

Demonstrating the lack of consensus on this issue, one urban liberal Catholic was very keen on a greater collaborative ministry between parishes, with more teams and groups, and preferably, team ministries. Unusually, one middle-of-the-road rural member of the clergy raised grass roots ecumenism as an issue related to this and pointed out that local communities expect the denominational barriers to break down at least as far as pastoral work is concerned. 'We share very much with a free church congregation and the Salvation Army. We hold surgery hours together with the doctor.' From Crewe, though, came the idea that the impending amalgamation of more parishes is like a kind of church Thatcherism. He could foresee that there would be: 'More church buildings and parochial work per clergyman, increasing emphasis on finances, strategies, audits (personal and parish), i.e. market forces.' It was unclear as to whether he was supporting these things as well as foreseeing them.

It seems from the survey that those favouring team ministries and rationalization do so as a reaction to the financial stresses rather than promoting them as good ideas independent of these. The feeling is that money will always be short, so perhaps there is an assumption that it will never be possible to save enough money, even if the Synodical structures and bureaucracies were to be abolished. Others favour a wholesale and radical change of the church structure for more sectarian reasons. This is what a radical Catholic from Camberwell had to say: '. . . most churches are clubs for the like-minded. This results from a sectarian church, increasingly obsessed with its own problems and intoxicated by its own fantasies.'

There is a general call for more non-stipendiary priests to take charge of parishes, as, in the words of a priest from an urban parish in Manchester:

> The present system is becoming unsustainable. There need to be new forms of ministry and closer co-operation with neighbouring parishes to share resources and expertise.

Perhaps backing up the argument that bishops should visit their clergy more often, a radical Evangelical from Lancashire described bishops as being '. . . too aloof and distant. There should be more bishops, more dioceses and they should scrap the purple shirt!'

An evangelical with an inner city parish in Manchester sees a wholly different scenario: the Church of England splitting. Initially this split would involve about a tenth of the clergy leaving because of women's ordination.

> This will increase the pressure to disestablish. If the church does disestablish, I can envisage a further pressure to form a more biblical, less episcopal church. I would welcome such a move, although I would prefer the Church of England to remain the national church. At a parish level, because of financial pressures and increasing lack of fifteen to forty year olds among the membership of many Church of England churches, the tendency will be towards merging the unsuccessful church with the more successful Evangelical traditional churches. To counter the obvious poaching tendencies of the more established and successful larger churches, I would prefer to see them using their increased membership and wealth to send out missionaries to support the smaller churches and encourage them to grow through intensive evangelism and biblical teaching.

Perhaps there is a warning here that if the enthusiasts are left to look after themselves, as they inevitably will do, they may set about church planting or poaching around in the community as their numbers grow. Would this be a good or a bad thing, though? As long as it does not affect the availability of the church to the 'unchurched' it can, presumably, do no harm.

A 'sacramentalist' from rural Northumberland had a particular word to say about the selection of clergy.

> The Church of England will not retain its spiritual authority within the nation until we are freed from the system

of selection and training imposed upon us by ACCM, which is an ecclesiastical bureaucracy to keep a certain type of person in authority within the church. This system, whereby the same kind of people continue in power, begins at the top and works through the system. We are swamped by pseudo-academics who talk about Christianity and theology with very poor practice. People with individuality and powers of leadership are an embarrassment, yet the country needs spiritual leadership from people having concern for the nation's soul and many people would respond.

Drawing, then, on the wide range of suggestions we have just read, I would put forward the view that the Church of England's priorities should be to retain the parish system, maintain sacred places, and have a trained minister available for everyone in the country, irrespective of their church membership allegiance or attendance. The enthusiasts will look after themselves. They will find their own places to meet and can be included within a broad Church of England with little difficulty; they are not the problem.

The problem is maintaining the availability of the church for the 'unchurched'. If the buildings are to be open to all for the big occasions and for quiet moments of reflection, there is no reason why they have to be maintained and owned by the Church of England. To keep every historic church open and guarantee its future, all historic religious buildings could be given over to a new national body that would keep them in trust. They should not just be monuments, but living places, open to all forms of community activity. They should be subjected to normal planning legislation and heritage controls and the faculty system should be abolished. It should be open for individuals to leave money to trust funds to maintain the buildings if they wish to, they would, in the main, be maintained on behalf of society by society and financed by means of grants from the Exchequer.

In Scotland, some great church buildings are owned by local authorities. The magnificent St Magnus Cathedral in Kirkwall, for instance, is owned by the Orkney Islands Council and yet used by the Church of Scotland for regular worship. There appears to be no contradiction in this. It is a facility freely available to all, funded by the community. After all, no one complains that English Heritage provides substantial grants to cathedrals. They amount to £4.5 million in 1993, with the single largest grant of £720 500 going to Lincoln. Since 1991, English Heritage has allocated £11.5 million to cathedrals and the total is expected to reach £19.5 million by 1995. English Heritage's fabric survey estimated that £185 million will have to be spent on Englands' cathedrals in this decade, and £85 million of this is eligible for grant aid.

Second, urban parish boundaries could be redrawn so that every part of an urban area is contained within a new parish of a manageable size. The size might be, on average, 3–4000 people and, on occasions, consist of just a couple of tower blocks or, on others, a whole estate. At present, a unit of ministry can range from 300 to 58 000. Not surprisingly, the smallest parish included in the survey was a rural one, and the largest a suburban parish in Hemel Hempstead. The former, in Surrey, was centred on a church more than 500 years old, had an electoral roll of 81 and an average Sunday attendance of over 50. By contrast, the suburban parish had an electoral roll of 900. It had, however, been divided into six districts to make ministry more practical.

In his book *The Myth of the Empty Church*, Professor Robin Gill described the case of the single incumbent looking after large numbers of small parishes as a recipe for long-term disaster. In this view he has been backed up by Leslie Francis in *Rural Anglicanism*. I would be in favour, therefore, of setting the ambitious aim that every parish should have its *own* minister. Some of the clergy would be paid a stipend and given a place to live, while others would be stipendiary clergy working for the church in other capacities, being given a small parish as well. Others might even be non-stipendiary clergy working in the community, again with a small parish to look after. They would, however, have had training and be the main point of contact for everyone. The size of a parish would have to be sufficiently small for the minister to be able to visit every household personally at least once every year and, certainly in urban areas, not every parish would have its church building. Indeed, in some urban areas there might only be a worshipping congregation of a dozen or two and there is no reason why they should not meet in homes or hire rooms at a community centre or club. Nevertheless, it would be possible for active members to periodically visit one of the more lively urban church buildings or go to the cathedral if it is nearby. In rural areas, the model should always be one parson for every church for every parish. If an individual church no longer has any form of population around it, it can be combined with another, but two churches would be the maximum. In some areas, there would be a stipendiary minister. Other rural parishes would provide part-time work for a retired clergyman. When my father retired in his sixties, he moved from running a group of churches serving a population of nearly 4000, to a small village in Devon with a population less than 400, and there worked as 'the vicar'. It was an ideal number and he knew and was known by everyone in the parish. He carried on working there until he was nearly eighty, giving an additional fifteen valuable years to his ministry.

Some have argued that clergy with rural charges have an easy life and if each only had one parish to be responsible for, their lives would be even easier. Following their recent study of 572 Anglican clergy, Douglas Davies, Charles Watkins and Michael Winter, wrote in *Church and Religion in Rural England* that most rural clergy felt just as fully occupied as their urban counterparts, working fifty-five to fifty-seven hours a week, of which half of the time was spent on 'sacerdotal' and 'pastoral' work. This means, one would deduce, that between twenty-five and thirty hours a week are spent on administration, fundraising and other duties that could easily be performed by the laity or even not undertaken at all.

In order to achieve this kind of cover, of one member of the clergy to each reasonably sized parish, there is no reason why the local reader or even church warden should not be ordained in order to be able to provide the sacraments in a small community. Given, too, that, shortly, there will be women priests to take up much of the additional work, there is no reason why there should be a shortage of clergy, as long as it is accepted that only about half of the active clergy will be working in the church as a full-time career and occupation. That this is possible is evidenced by the Norwich diocese, which has already opted for a local, non-stipendiary ministry scheme, largely for financial reasons.

Concerns have, however, been expressed that such an option could lead to a two-tier priesthood, as the kind of training that might be possible at a local level cannot hope to match that of a full-time theological college course. This could be the case as far as academic or theological studies are concerned, but there is no reason why local men or women ordained for local ministry might not continue their theological studies for many years after ordination through home study, Open University courses, and other forms of part-time education. It must be asked, too, what level of academic expertise should be required of our clergy. There must be many people for whom academic work is difficult, yet who have an excellent grasp of what is required in terms of pastoral work—the right sympathetic touch plus a true sense of reverence when celebrating the sacraments. Why should these people be excluded from the local unpaid ministry?

The idea that non-stipendiary ministers might be treated as second class was raised in a letter to the *Church Times* by John Mantle, the Vice-Principal of the Canterbury School of

Ministry. He wrote, 'the fact is that I have already witnessed highly trained general non-stipendiary ministers shamefully treated as second class by their fellow clergy.' Earlier in this letter he had asked:

> whatever happened to the concept of lay ministry? The answer is that it is still around, but it doesn't fit in with our understanding of Eucharistic presidency. The church is not necessarily short of ministers, that is, leaders of worship and those who pastorally care: our pews are full of them. So, don't we have a case for seriously considering episcopal permission for extending communion, or, dare we suggest it, occasional lay celebration?

Whether local people going forward for ordination will actually be accepted by the selectors, however, is a matter that some people are concerned about. Robert Leach, reviewing the week in the *Church of England Newspaper* on 18 June 1993 told the story of a woman he had known for many years, with a lifetime's dedicated service to the church, who offered herself for ordination to work in the parish.

> She was unanimously and enthusiastically supported by the parish, which had been identified as needing a second clergyman.
> However, after a few brief interviews, she was turned down. The inevitable letter to the bishop prompted the inevitable reply; those who met her three times know her better than those of us who have only known her and worked with her for a third of a century.
> Anyone looking at who has been rejected and who has been accepted for ordination share my views that selection boards and bishops may as well draw names out of a hat for all the good their present procedures are.

To return to an analysis of the roles clergy might perform; in each diocese, a group of senior stipendiary ministers can have an overseeing responsibility for groups of parishes, to ensure that there is adequate cover if a clergyman falls ill, and so would perform a role somewhere between that of a rural dean and an archdeacon.

At diocesan level, there would still be a bishop, but his (or, eventually, her) duties would change. The prime duty would be to travel around parishes visiting the clergy and congregations. If he or she was to spend, on average, four days a week out and about, there is no reason why each congregation could not be visited frequently and on a regular basis. The bishop would then get a true hands-on feel for the diocese, the clergy would no longer feel isolated, and the congregations would get to know their 'shepherd'.

The diocesan cathedral would remain as an historical shop window for Christianity in the community; a place for visitors and others to come to, and a special place in which the great diocesan ceremonies and services could be held.

In this scheme of things, in contrast to some proposals that the deaneries should be the budget-holders and key units of organization, I can see no role for deaneries, let alone deanery synods. Also, I see no reason why, at diocesan level, the ordained clergy and other activists need meet more than twice a year for a day at a time. On these occasions there need be no formal agenda or legislative business; it could be a day of worship, study, and a way of getting to know each other. I find it hard too to see a role for archdeacons as most of the administrative work that presently comes their way could be undertaken by lay specialists.

As for the General Synod, it would not survive in its present form. Twice a year, the bishops, representative clergy and laity from each diocese would meet—once at the campus at York University and once at the university campus of Canterbury. Church House, Westminster could be sold.

The General Synod's role as a legislative body would be radically amended. The biennial meetings would be opportunities to debate broad policy outlines and discuss wider issues of the day. The income from the Church Commissioners would, after the radically reduced central expenses had been taken from it, be distributed on a per capita basis to the dioceses to spend. Clergy would be paid at an appropriate diocesan level, selected at diocesan level, and trained locally wherever possible. Interestingly, there is currently a great debate within the Church of England about the future of its theological colleges and there are proposals to rationalize and close certain of them. An idea that might be more appropriate to the church of the future is that there should be *more* training centres, linked with a local university, each receiving fewer students, but each, because of their links with another place of education, costing far less to run. Indeed, there is no reason why training for the ministry should involve long periods of residential study. The new colleges, then, could be far more accommodating to the needs of part-time ordinands.

Another way forward would be to give maximum encouragement for local parishes and dioceses to co-operate with other churches and denominations. There is no reason why buildings should not be shared by Anglicans, the free churches and Roman Catholics. However, when asked about sharing buildings or facilities, only 12 per cent of the parish clergy surveyed said that they did, with 85 per cent saying they never did, although one clergyman from an urban parish in the Midlands said that he would be glad to do so. On the other hand a clergyman from a parish in Exeter on the edge of the city expressed the view that various pressures on other clergy made such co-operation difficult. A rural clergyman, though, from Hampshire said that there were no places of worship for other denominations in his three parishes and as a result many non-Anglicans came to the Church of England services.

All things considered, it would make sense to increase the practice of sharing buildings. For example, there are many dwindling free church congregations struggling to maintain large and inappropriate buildings, many of which have little historical or architectural merit. Just keeping the roof from leaking is a major undertaking and call on resources, while heating these buildings for what are often just a few church attenders is a regular winter nightmare. Similarly, there are Roman Catholic congregations that rely on finding halls or hiring school rooms in order to meet. It would make a great deal of sense, therefore, if the one parish church owned by the community was used by *all* Christians. The buildings would be easier to heat economically and no single congregation would have to bear the full cost of maintenance. Each denomination or church would have its own time on a Sunday and there would be the added bonus that all would be more likely to meet from time to time for collective acts of worship. Weddings and funerals could be conducted by the priests or ministers of any of the churches, depending on the wishes of those involved. As a result, local patterns of co-operation would evolve and the whole cumbersome central negotiating movement towards church unity would be wound up and real ecumenical progress would be made at grass roots level.

The whole purpose of such an exercise in reconstruction would be to rid the church of its cumbersome bureaucracy, enable dioceses and parishes to thrive, keep places of worship open to all, and set, as the prime target, the availability of a minister, pastor and priest for every parish.

The question of how bishops should be selected in future, then, is a critical one. There is no doubt that, when reviewing the bench of bishops from the gallery at the General Synod, there is an astonishing uniformity in their grey suits and grey minds. A few individuals stand out, but most seem to have been selected with the help of some kind of episcopal identikit set. At present, bishops are selected, not, as they once were, by the Prime Minister and a secret inner committee of advisers, but by a hybrid process in which the established appointments system contributes ideas to a special committee that includes representatives of the diocese and Synod and then two names are put forward to the

Queen for selection. The Queen is expected, or rather the Prime Minister in her name is expected, to choose the first of the two names. At least once, though, Mrs Thatcher decided to go for the second in order to avoid a well-known radical bishop being appointed to a senior diocesan post and found, to her chagrin, that she had chosen as number two an equally radical individual.

Prime ministers have taken varying degrees of interest in the appointments of bishops, but one of the most conscientious was Edward Heath, an active Anglican. When he was Prime Minister, he expected forms to be filled out by the diocese stating their requirements. Every diocese he heard from appeared to want a man aged between forty-four and forty-eight who was married with four children (preferably two at university and two still at school) and with a knowledge both of agriculture and industry. The only difference, Mr Heath says, that ever arose was that a diocese with a High Church bishop wanted his replacement to be a little lower while a diocese with a Low Church bishop wanted one a little higher.

The system of selection adopted by many other Anglican provinces has an equal number of drawbacks. When the first woman bishop was elected at a meeting of the Massachusetts diocese in Boston, USA, a system of single transferable votes was adopted, and voting by Synod members went into many ballots. In between ballots, there was more lobbying than prayer, with some quite malicious rumours being circulated in order to promote one candidate or defame another.

The message from these examples is clear: the danger of leaving the selection of bishops to the English system is that a depressing uniformity emerges. One of the criticisms in the famous preface in *Crockford's Clerical Directory* preface was that Archbishop Runcie had given preferment through his influence to many of his old pals with St Albans and Cuddesdon connections. It was an unfair criticism, but one which had emerged as an inevitable consequence of the process. On the other hand, if too wide an electorate is involved, then all sorts of curious and irrational preferences will shape the final choice. Perhaps it should be left to each diocese to choose the right person for their particular area, but candidates could be nominated from a central pool of suitable people.

Clearly the bishop of today needs to be someone who is at home handling committees and dealing with paperwork. The bishop of the future, however, ought to be someone good at dealing with people at a pastoral level, as once the administrative burden has been lifted this is the role that the bishop should fulfil. He or she needs to be a person who can inspire and encourage, rather than one who can ensure that diocesan returns have been sent to Church House on time. What is amazing is that, despite the various systems adopted by provinces in the Anglican Communion around the world, as well as the dull and uninspiring, some men have emerged who have transparent and obvious ability and there have been few utterly disastrous appointments (depending, of course, on how one defines disastrous: the efficient bureaucrat who gets everything completed in triplicate on time but never visits the parish and is utterly uninspiring, could be said to be more disastrous than the bishop who gets himself into trouble with the tabloid press).

One can look to other provinces within the Anglican Communion, too, for ideas as to how to reform the church's general structures. There is substantial growth in many parts of Africa, where priests and bishops frequently emerge from their communities and, often, with the minimum of formal training, are immensely successful in leading thriving congregations. Many are people of great courage and face real persecution. Many, too, lead austere lives, being forced by the economic conditions of their own countries to suffer alongside their people. In the USA, too, there is another, though quite different, structure that could be the model. There, an affluent church has high status and total autonomy. Some of the episcopal churches' congregations are hundreds strong, entirely self-supporting, and give generously to charity. Yet, no matter how far one searches world-wide, no model, however inspiring, is entirely appropriate for the Church of England because of its unique status as the established national church.

A radical and new approach has to be taken in England and there are no convenient precedents to draw on. It can only be hoped that whatever changes *are* made align with the key aim that the church remains the church for all of the nation. That changes *have* to be made is undeniable, if only for financial reasons. Since the recent loss by the Church Commissioners of £800 million of church assets in bad property investments during the recession, the church faces financial crisis. The Church of Scotland should serve as a warning in this regard. It is a few years ahead of England in its decline, and its long-standing financial crisis now borders on insolvency.

For most of the centuries of its existence, the Church of England had little central organization as the communications systems of the country made this impossible, so bishops ruled in their dioceses. The problems faced by the Church of England today are very similar to those faced by other large organizations covering huge geographical areas. The central organization takes on a life of its own and the roots that fed it originally begin to wither. The European Community discovered subsidiarity as the solution. 'Devolution' is a vogue word in government circles. The Church of England needs to review ways of bolstering its national role by reinvigorating the parishes and slimming down its central bureaucracy.

5

Heritage and the New Folk-Faith

Just opposite the King's School entrance to Canterbury Cathedral, there is a 'New Age' emporium. It sells tarot cards, books on the signs of the zodiac and crystal balls.

In Glastonbury, in Somerset, once the heart of Christianity in the region, with its monastery, holy sights and tales of Joseph of Aremathea, New Age shops are everywhere for Glastonbury is the mecca for those who have swallowed whole the myth and magic of the New Age movement. It is a place which has taken upon itself the mantle of a super-sacred place. It is where mythical ley lines converge, where earth powers come to the surface, where magic happens in the mind.

Some people would argue that this is the place where, if anything is to be found which has superseded the folk-faith of the nation, it is to be had there. Yet, there is, possibly, a stronger case for arguing that the *real* folk religion of today is to be found at Comet and B and Q and Tesco where new congregations gather on Sundays to worship the Gods of Mammon. But while that *is* an overwhelming interest, it is *not* a faith. Underlying consumerism there is nothing of any spiritual substance in it.

A faith is what provides answers to those questions everyone has to face at least once in a lifetime. Many people will pass many years without a single political thought or macro-economic question crossing their minds, but everyone has to address spiritual questions. When a person they love dies, when they fall in love for the first time, when they face serious illness or even death, spiritual questions rush into the mind. What is the purpose of life, where have we come from, where are we going to, is there a God?

Some ready answers to these questions are found in the half-baked interpretations of such concepts as reincarnation, auras, karma, and so on that have travelled across the ocean from America. Although it is very hard to encapsulate what all these ideas actually mean, if they have one theme in common it is an acknowledgement that human beings are also spiritual beings, that the spiritual nature of humanity is, somehow, it is suggested, capable of being in tune with the seasons, planet earth and mother nature in a way which we in this modern age have tended to forget. The Christian festivals have, in the main, taken over from the pre-Christian festivals of the year, but there is still a longing to be in touch with something that is non-material. There is a vague but unexpressed feeling that, in some way, the Christian religion has played a part in the development of materialism. The Protestant work ethic, after all, produced the Industrial Revolution. It is argued, too, that in some Protestant traditions there is a theology of acquisition. Even when studying the creation, some Christians emphasize the notion of the dominion of mankind over the other creatures, as if to say that all creation has been put there by a God for the benefit of the human race to do with as it wishes. There is a feeling, too, that the feminine has been ignored. The world consists of male *and* female and yet, somehow, Christians have traditionally referred to God as a man and the feminine, the mother side of creation, has been neglected. Yet these ideas are only held by a minority in their entirety.

Pre-Christian ideas surface in ways that, perhaps, are not recognized as such, but are very much alive. Bonfire night and Hallowe'en, in the dark days of Autumn, coincide with the dates in the Christian calendar on which All Souls and All Saints are remembered. In other words, Christians use those times of year to remember the dead. In British folk-faith, however, the dead are remembered rather differently: children dress up as witches and ghouls, and ghost stories are told. Around Britain a wide range of other folk customs have also survived through the mists of time and are still re-enacted. Many of them involve the symbolic use of fire, others refer to the Devil, and there are fertility rites connected with the farming cycle. Few of these customs show signs of decline—indeed, many grow in significance and popularity year by year. Yet, even if few people are consciously aware of the old folk-faith mysteries as they play Hallowe'en games or light bonfires, many do recognize the overt paganism in other common practices. A large number of people openly accept some parts of New Age or revived pre-Christian thinking. The horoscope is a popular item in most newspapers, for example, there is an acceptance of the possibility of reincarnation, and a range of superstitions are followed with care. Even town planners will often omit the number thirteen when numbering houses on a new street. Also, according to one survey of 2000 12 to 18 year olds compiled by the Christian Research Association, 1 in 3 of those surveyed admitted to having experimented with occult practices such as the ouija board. About a million secondary school pupils in Britain have had some contact with ouija boards, astrology, or tarot cards, and 10 per cent of those interviewed who described themselves as Christians have been interested in astrology.

Many superstitions also concern the traditional rites of passage—weddings and funerals. Couples still like the idea of getting married in the country church with the bride wearing white, attractive bridesmaids attending, a choir, a sunny day, and bells ringing. Such a wedding is part of a folk memory of an idyllic past. Many sacrifices are made in order to afford this ideal, but often couples find an unwillingness on the part of churches—they do not want to become mere stage sets for social occasions. Even if a church service is held, many of the 'unchurched' find the new form of marriage service unfamiliar and lacking the poetry of the old. So, new traditions are growing up that equal or surpass that of the role of the church. They are practices and traditions which can be followed to make a wedding an event even if the ceremony is conducted at a drab register office. The little superstitions become important. For instance, it is unlucky for the bridegroom to see the bride in her wedding dress before the big day. There is even the ritual of getting the bridegroom drunk on his stag night. Friends tie old tins to and spray shaving foam messages on the car for going away. The set speeches at the wedding reception, the cutting of the cake, and the reading of the messages have become important parts of the new ritual, as have toasting the bridesmaids and making sure that the bride is wearing something old, something new, something borrowed and something blue. The photographer, too, plays a key role. Once the vicar doubled as the master of ceremonies, but often today it is the man with the camera who organizes and gives form to the day.

On the subject of marriage, the survey tested two potential areas of division within the church: the issue of its willingness to marry couples where one or both of the partners has or have previously been divorced, and its willingness to provide some form of service, equivalent to the marriage service, for homosexual couples, making public vows of their dedication and love to each other.

The survey produced the following result: 61 per cent of clergy said that they would be prepared to marry couples where one partner has been divorced, but 32 per cent, though permitted to do so, would not. Additional comments volunteered included, 'under very strict limits, with careful preparation, by no means all comers', 'I do if they are regular worshipping members', 'depends entirely on circumstances, Jesus was not rigid', and 'I see no difference in marrying divorcees or marrying non-Christians!'

On the issue of conducting a service of blessing for a homosexual couple, only 14 per cent of clergy were prepared to do so, with 76 per cent being firmly against the idea. Associated comments included, 'yes under certain circumstances and upon enquiry', 'no, marriage is a sacrament, homosexual relations are not', and 'not as a public rite.'

It could be said that these are marginal issues, important to a few, but not so important when it comes to the way the church is perceived generally. Nevertheless, with an increasing divorce rate, the willingness of the clergy to be prepared to marry a couple where one or other has been divorced is fast becoming a crucial issue. The church that entirely rules out the marriage of a couple where one has been divorced automatically excludes a substantial number of the 'unchurched'. The popular compromise now is for there to be a church blessing following a register office legal ceremony.

The other major rite of passage, funerals, however are losing even the touches of folk-faith. They are sombre occasions in bleak crematoria where everyone is a little embarrassed and no one knows what to do. These are a far cry from the traditional funeral under the ageless yew tree in the parish churchyard where, for centuries, the Christian church and folk-faith happily coexisted.

I have attended funerals that have been a profound occasion for a whole community. I remember from my time living in Orkney how an island funeral had a solemnity and a purpose to it which I have seldom seen further south. The minister in black, the mourners in their best suits, the graveside overlooking the sea, the wind and, probably the rain— it all had an eternal feel to it. Most people at the graveside knew each other, they were members of the same community. However, frequently, a funeral in the south of England involves disparate circles of friends or acquaintances of the person who died getting together and not recognizing or knowing each other. Sometimes members of the family who have not seen each other for months or years turn up and try to make polite conversation.

Funerals and weddings, though, are occasions when the Christian church has its greatest opportunity to take its message to the non-churchgoers. It must do so by example rather than by preaching. The Reverend Jack Burton, the Methodist minister best known as being the bus driver minister from Norwich, says that, for almost twenty-five years, his pastoral ministry has been directed almost entirely towards the needs of non-churchgoers. Of taking a funeral he writes in his book *The Gap*: 'Dignity, warmth, sensitivity, and imagination are what is required—though gesture, symbol and colour *are* important.' He reflects on what he describes as the unusual opportunity which has fallen to him to provide over many years:

> a sanctuary of holiness and tranquillity and to supply various forms of religion-on-demand which I call folk religion. If we believe, as I do, that all God's children have the right to worship the heavenly father, they also have the right to expect the help of His servants in the preparation and presentation of worship. Their requests should be welcomed and dealt with seriously and generously, unless we are content to see ourselves as members of an exclusive, favoured *sect*, which is a far cry from the grand, all-embracing, Trinitarian faith of the Holy Catholic church.

Jack Burton is, thus, willing to welcome any suggestions by families to introduce any ideas, however neo-pagan they may appear, into weddings and funerals. Better that he, as a Christian minister, is at the centre than that the funeral becomes merely the disposal of a body by a team of professional undertakers.

What society's folk-faith has not, however, found a replacement for is the christening. One superstition that has not survived is that concerning the fate of a child's soul if he or she dies unbaptized, although there are occasions in hospitals when babies who are seriously ill are baptized by nurses feeling that this is the right thing to do. Often, however, there is more of a feeling that a child needs a name. Maybe the equivalent of a christening is now the registration of the child's birth, although that is a very formal and not at all special transaction. The old-fashioned christening, in which the family turn up in their best clothes at the church, is on the decline. One reason for this is that many clergy are unhappy about baptizing children of parents who are themselves not churchgoers. It is felt that the parents need to be involved and that christening is a declaration of intent as to how a child is going to be brought up, not simply a welcome to the world by the world. As the survey shows, there are some churches where children will not be baptized unless the parents are regular churchgoers and, in almost every case, parents are given a talk by the clergyman beforehand to encourage, if not require them, to bring the child up in a Christian home. Not surprisingly, infant baptism fell from 40 per cent to 28 per cent of live births in England between 1980 and 1990.

An additional piece of evidence suggesting that membership of the Church of England is becoming an adult decision, like the joining of many other denominations is, rather than something which happens as a matter of course, can be found by looking at what has happened to confirmations.

An analysis of confirmation numbers over nine years in the diocese of Chelmsford reported in the *Church of England Newspaper* in June 1993, revealed two growing trends. The number of candidates for confirmation was rapidly declining—by 15 per cent in one three-year period—with fewer teenagers than ever before, coming forward to affirm the baptismal vows. 'If confirmation remains targeted as a teenage rite of passage, it seems inevitable that the number of candidates will continue to fall', the report says, and it reveals that an increasing proportion of candidates asking to be confirmed are adults. Instead of being aimed at under-twenty years olds, most of the resources available should now be targeted at adults, they say. Further, a report by the

Heritage and the New Folk-Faith

Reverend Professor Leslie Francis and David Lankshear of the National Society came up with what the *Church of England Newspaper* described as a bizarre conclusion:

> The benefices which present a number of pre-teenagers for confirmation can expect small average congregations, fewer participants in each group and less overall income than congregational benefices which do not present young candidates for confirmation.

It could be argued that one of the reasons the modern generation does not need regular contact with the church in order to be able to meet its spiritual needs is that these needs can be met on a day-to-day basis via the broadcast media. By this is meant, not that they are watching *Songs of Praise* or listening to the daily service on the radio, but that music is now widely available.

While it might not generally be recognized as such or always described in these words, listening to great music can be a spiritual experience. Music is non-material, ethereal, non-verbal, and has a very direct way of touching the soul and the emotions. When the greatest composers wanted to write their greatest music, they chose the vehicle of the mass to do so. For centuries, before recorded music became available, the churches knew the power of music. They retained and commissioned the great composers and musicians to produce work for the glory of God and to induce in those at church an experience of eternity. Today, composers still write religious works. For example, after years of producing one hit musical after another, the composer Sir Andrew Lloyd Webber wanted to make his mark as a serious composer and chose a religious theme. Modern composers like John Taverner also talk of being inspired by their spiritual search and faith. Millions of people now find that they no longer need to go to church, but instead tune in to Classic FM or Radio 3 for an instant spiritual uplift. The great advantage of music is that it is religion without dogma. To be moved by Bach's B minor mass, or Stainer's

Crucifixion, or Elgar's *Dream of Gerontius*, or Mozart's *Requiem* does not require the listener to subscribe to a creed. Similarly, religious art is now open to all. *The Last Supper*, *The Last Judgement*, Michelangelo's *David*, Grant Sutherland's Coventry tapestry, and all the art to be found in the great cathedrals may be seen and the messages absorbed without having to go further into theology, without needing to make any commitment of faith. Films and musicals, too, have had religious themes, ranging from *The Last Temptation of Christ* through to *Jesus Christ Superstar*. Many in their time have been condemned by the mainstream churches and, yet, all have lent insight into spiritual matters that have been picked up by non-churchgoers. There was one particular scene in *The Last Temptation of Christ*, a film roundly condemned by all Christian leaders as blasphemous, in which that obscure Christian phrase concerning the blood of the lamb was brought to life and given meaning. It was a cut from the sacrificial slaughter of a lamb and its blood dripping into a bowl, to Christ picking up a bowl at the last supper and drinking the red wine from it.

Christians who believe that their spiritual obligations consist of reading the Bible, their daily prayer, and worshipping with a community of like-minded folk within the four walls of a church on a Sunday, are missing out on a rainbow of opportunity that the non-churchgoers make full use of. My impression is that as a church grows numerically, the theology and scope of interpretation often narrow. Thus, what goes on within the four walls of a church on a Sunday is becoming increasingly strange and alien to the non-churchgoers outside. There was a time when the church was part of the community and represented the spiritual life of the nation, when everyone, no matter how infrequently they went there, knew something of what went on in a church. They knew most of the hymns and most of the prayers. There is now, however, a widening gulf between what goes on in church and what goes on outside. It is interesting to see how that gulf involves some people becoming almost two personalities. During the week, there are many who are involved in science, business or technology, free-thinking and well-paid, who, on Sundays, revert to a narrow form of thinking quite at odds with the world that they know the other six days of the week.

At times of community disaster, however, there still remains sufficient residual folk-faith for the church to play a prominent role in expressing collective grief. The hundreds of people, entirely 'unchurched' and unfamiliar with any form of ritual or spiritual expression, who were struck by the tragedy of the Hillsborough disaster took to the cathedral to express their anguish. The invitation by the bishop to a service which would be held there shortly after the disaster was taken up with enthusiasm. It was the obvious and the only place to which they could repair. One of the reporters present noticed how the young people were dressed. The women were either dressed colourfully and extravagantly in their very best, or in small, skimpy black numbers.

> They'd obviously sought advice as to what to wear, what was appropriate, and that advice came from their grandmothers. You wore your best or you wore black. For them their best was what they wore to party and that which was black was not designed for mourning. According to the fashion of the time, it tended to be short and skimpy.

Another instance of when the church finds itself taking a key role at a time of public grief is when a whole community is horrified or galvanized by an evil or crime. The church at the local level is at the centre of the way in which people respond. The Reverend Peter Tilley is the Rector of St Mary's, Walton, on Merseyside. Just yards from his church, the body of the little murdered boy James Bulger was discovered. In Mr Tilley's words, 'the phone rarely stopped ringing during the days following the tragedy.' He was able to witness the 'enormous levels of support and concern to have come out of the tragedy.' He remarked of his 'faith in people's strength to pull through.' Through the Liverpool Diocese Board of Social Responsibility, a leaflet was distributed on 'coping with the aftermath of the Warrington bomb', another tragic incident that occurred near to the parish. 'People have had the stuffing ripped out of them,' Mr Tilley said in an interview in the *Church Times* in April 1993, 'but the tide will turn. And when it does, people must have something ahead of them to believe in. Meanwhile, the church must be out there building up that faith.'

Also shortly after the Warrington bombing, the Archbishop of Canterbury went to the town to join the Bishop of Warrington, the Right Reverend Michael Henshall, for, at times like these, the church not only has a pastoral role in comforting the dying and bereaved, it also has to be on hand to deal with anger. The anger can be directed along spiritual lines: why does God let this happen, how can he be a God of love, what is the purpose of life if such terrible things can happen?

In an article published in the *Church of England Newspaper* in March 1993, Canon Christopher Hill, Precentor of St Paul's Cathedral, wrote that cathedrals provide a context in which people can face themselves and the questions that really matter. He quoted the experience of the novelist Susan Howatch, who, he says, was 'your average nominal Anglican' when she began to write, married to an atheist, non-agnostic but not a practising Christian either. She writes of her own rediscovery of herself in the Christian faith at the time when she was hugely successful professionally. She also recalls the failure of her marriage.

I was not at peace. I was too conscious of the fact that making money and being a success as a novelist had left me unfulfilled and unhappy. It was then as my private world became increasingly dark, that the light began to seep from the cathedral. [She was referring to Salisbury Cathedral, having just moved into the close to live.] That extraordinary building, which I had until then viewed perfunctorily as a mere beautiful landmark, suddenly started to infiltrate my consciousness on a variety of unexpected levels. I gazed at the Cathedral and the Cathedral gazed back. It occurred to me that I did not know quite so much about the important things of life as I thought I did. Then I realized that I knew absolutely nothing about anything and that it was high time I stopped wasting my life and started trying to find answers to the questions I had always been too busy to ask. 'Who was I, what was I supposed to be doing with my life, what did it all mean, if anything?'

I gazed again at the Cathedral and now I saw beyond the beautiful façade the creation of supreme value which had been achieved by hundreds of people who had used their special gifts not to glorify themselves, but to glorify God.

This insight encouraged me to reason that if I were to postulate the existence of God (a most unsettling step for someone who had never paid God much attention), and if I were to theorize that he had created each individual to play a specific role in his creation, my task was obviously to find out what role had been assigned to me and then play that role to the hilt in order to move into harmony with my creator, and thus into harmony with the human pattern which was myself.

Canon Hill wrote:

the Cathedral for Susan Howatch was a catalyst for her self-discovery, and the rediscovery of God. And it is this theme which underlies her six Church of England novels. Self-discovery and the rediscovery of God.

As a canon of St Paul's I believe that our cathedrals, their architecture, their music and their worship, can also be catalysts for a voyage of self-discovery and the encounter with the God who is part of our being.

Canon Hill talks to thousands of people who are drawn to
the magnificent architecture of St Paul's and mentions how
he encourages visitors to gaze up in silent wonder, as Susan
Howatch had gazed at Salisbury Cathedral and see if her
questions about herself and God do not also occur to them.

> You don't need many words to wonder at the mystery
> and glory of God as reflected in the grandeur of St Paul's.
> It's a natural next step to invite them to consider their
> place in the context of this glory and grandeur.
>
> But human beings are rational creatures and this
> means that we need to articulate our praise to God,
> however stuttering and inadequate our words may be.
> This takes us from the architecture of cathedrals to their
> worship and especially the choral worship which is the
> cathedral's distinctive and unique tradition.

Canon Hill then went on to describe how Susan Howatch
became a regular attender at worship:

> To be present at such an act of worship can provide not
> only an opening of our eyes and ears to great architec-
> ture and music, but it can also open our hearts to the
> God to whom the building and its music point and give
> glory. And, like Susan Howatch, in finding a cathedral,
> we may also begin to find our true selves.

The case for the role of cathedrals could not have been
put better. All the great cathedrals—their architecture and
their music—are immediate points of contact which the
'unchurched' can relate to without needing to use words.
Words might even be a stumbling block, particularly when
they require commitment as even those expressing faith can
become too precise and too legalistic, which is offputting to
those not willing to make a commitment in the orthodox
way. Cathedrals, too, have a certain anonymity to them that
the 'unchurched' find puts them more at ease. A person can
wander into a cathedral and no one demands to know who
they are; no one wants to shake them warmly by the hand

and welcome them to the club. They are, instead, places of private devotion, and most cathedrals keep a quiet chapel aside where people can share their thoughts with God. To visit a great cathedral and hear evensong being sung in the distance is an act of individual devotion and can be a spiritual experience which does not require words—they would, in fact, threaten to shatter the harmony.

Cathedrals also have a great role to play as the set piece venues for great acts of worship, when churchgoers from around the diocese can come and celebrate what unites them. These events also serve as the church's outreach to those many thousands who do not want to be part of an enthusiastic denomination. There are many thousands like Susan Howatch who rediscover a faith without going to church and, on the way, do so by absorbing the heritage.

Westminster Abbey is probably the best known of all the great churches in Britain and it is there that events take place which identify the Church of England with national identity and values and the folk-faith they incorporate. However, will it be possible for the Church of England to maintain its role as a national church, available to all, if it becomes disestablished? Are not the two functions and roles inextricably linked? A distinction surely has to be drawn between the role of the church as a repository and expression of folk-faith and that where it is merely used as a totem of the State.

Forty years ago when the Queen was crowned in Westminster Abbey, the church was much involved. The ceremony had mystical and spiritual qualities to it that lent a divine authority to the role of monarch. Being the Queen's ministers, the Government of the day basks in that reflected divine glory, and, with the authority of St Paul to back them up, can make the claim that they are God's representatives or magistrates on earth, and, therefore, the people should obey the Government. However, if the church shed this role and relieved the Queen of her position as supreme Governor of the Church of England, and required her to remove from her coinage the letters DG, which imply that she rules by the grace of God, the church could still perform its national pastoral role. It would not have to splinter into hundreds of small, enthusiastic groups, cast off and cut off from the population at large.

Constitutionally, the Church of England could then adopt a role something akin to the one adopted by the Church of Scotland. For there although the Queen is not the head of the Church of Scotland, she undertakes to uphold the rights of the Presbyterian church, and the Lord High Commissioner, her representative, attends the general assembly of the Church of Scotland to watch that the church does nothing of which the Queen would disapprove. Using this arrangement as a model, perhaps the government, in whatever form, could guarantee the independence and rights of the Church of England without necessarily having any control over it. The church would then be free to set about establishing the new parochial structure that would be required to ensure that everyone could call on it when they needed to.

Such a separation would also enable changes to take place within the monarchy itself. No longer could the monarch claim that he or she is in a position of authority by divine right—an authority which is anyway beginning to wear very thin. The nation at large sees the extravagant privileges enjoyed by the monarch and the breakdown of family life evident within the royal family and is not impressed. In future, for instance, an option could be for the monarch as a person to be dispensed with and for a more impersonal concept of the Crown to be introduced as a focus of national loyalty. However, the abolition of the monarchy is not required for disestablishment to take place, although, if the monarchy was abolished, disestablishment would be an inevitable consequence.

A simple form of disestablishment could involve constitutional changes that need not have any great impact on the ordinary person in the pew. Such a change could simply be a confirmation of the Church of England's role as the major church in the land rather than its national church. The constitutional changes would involve, for instance, the church taking upon itself through the synodical or other self-governing structures all responsibilities for its organization. It would no longer be necessary for church legislation to be debated and passed by Parliament, and the remaining political involvement in the appointment of bishops could be removed. Many members of the Church of England would welcome such increased autonomy, yet, at the same time, certain privileges would be lost. The trade-off would undoubtedly result in the withdrawal of bishops from the House of Lords, and in changes to such things as planning regulations, with the church being required to submit all proposed changes to buildings to local authorities.

The results of the survey suggest that at least half the clergy feel that the church still gains more from its special constitutional status than it loses. When asked by the survey, 'Would you favour the disestablishment of the Church of England?', 39 per cent of clergy responded with a 'yes', while 50 per cent said 'no'.

As for the 'unchurched', the special position held by the Church of England offers a certain reassurance, that access to the church is a right that goes with citizenship, so this right would undoubtedly be seriously undermined if the Church of England renounced its special role. One only has to witness the way in which MPs express strong views about the church and its business, even when they are not practising members of it, to see how many British people believe the Church of England to be their church. Indeed, attempts earlier this century to revise the prayer-book were defeated in Parliament with many agnostics and members of other churches voting and taking part in the debates.

Changing the status of the Church of England would, therefore, require great delicacy if it were successfully to lose the encumbrances of being established but still retain the advantages. Change is, however, more likely to come about not as a well-planned exercise, but as a crisis response to some future royal upheaval or scandal.

6
The Ordination
of Women

When the result of the historic General Synod vote in November 1992 was announced, only a suppressed gasp of delight from a group of women in clerical black in the gallery broke the silence and solemnity of the occasion. Outside, however, things were very different. As soon as the news broke, the large crowd of members of the Movement for the Ordination of Women gathering on the green outside Church House, Westminster, broke into cheering. Women who had battled for this moment for many years hugged each other and wept. The bright lights of the television cameras caught the atmosphere.

As the General Synod broke up, huddles of defeated traditionalists were seen in corners debating what to do next, and, later, the opponents of the move silently made their way home.

To many traditionalists, the decision by the Synod (carried by a margin substantially greater than a simple majority, although by only a narrow margin constitutionally) was the straw that broke the camel's back. For example, the Conservative MP Anne Widdecombe felt that, from that moment, she was no longer a member of the Church of England—the church in which she had been born and brought up. By the spring, she had made public her move to the Roman Catholic church, and, in a highly publicized ceremony, she was received into that church.

At the same time, John Gummer, without announcing a decision to join the Roman Catholics, only that he had resigned from the Synod, wrote in *The Tablet* that the Church of England could no longer claim to be a national church: 'The General Synod is busy with the privatization of the Church of England. The Church which the Elizabethan Settlement sought to make the Church of the English nation is turning itself into a sect.'

Arguably, John Gummer is right. The Church of England, for many reasons, has ceased to be the natural repository of the spiritual values of the nation, yet, of all those reasons, the least likely was the one given later in his article. In a direct reference to the Synod's decision to allow the ordination of women to the priesthood, John Gummer wrote:

> Very soon you will not be able to be a member of the Church of England unless you are prepared to believe as an article of faith that the General Synod can, by a two-thirds majority, alter the orders and doctrines of the church . . . This Synod-driven church has sought to alienate the good will and assets of the Church of the nation and assign them to a body made up only of people who are prepared to assent to this novel doctrine of the infallibility of the General Synod.

Mr Gummer had hit the wrong nail firmly on the head. By and large, the theological arguments about the ordination of women to the priesthood leave the majority of nominal Anglicans cold. To them it is little more than the modern equivalent of the old medieval debate about how many angels can dance on the end of a pin. Some, like active Anglicans who have dressed up their objections in theological arguments to give them a greater respectability, have deeper reasons to be opposed to the idea. Some even have problems concerning their own attitudes to women, resulting from their upbringing, cultural background, or even their own sexuality, and a general unease about women taking roles of responsibility. However, a substantial number of people, especially from the younger generation, who have never known a king on the throne, have grown used to being treated by women doctors, employed by women bosses, and who have lived for twelve years with a government headed by a woman prime minister, fail to see any reason why a woman should *not* be a priest. Indeed, in recent years, many nominal Anglicans have attended baptisms, weddings, and funerals conducted by women deacons who, from all outward appearances, have to them been women priests. Overwhelmingly, my impression from the parishes is that, once a woman deacon becomes known for her pastoral work, objections to the ordination of women to the priesthood melt away.

Women deacons are becoming increasingly familiar in a whole range of church appointments. There are now at least seventeen honorary canons and two residential canons (at Portsmouth and Sheffield) who are women. In the St Albans diocese, there is an interesting case of a woman deacon married to a vicar who has now taken a parish from her husband, who has gone into semi-retired non-stipendiary ministry. While her husband, the Reverend Ray Williams, remains legally the incumbent, as he has been for twelve years, Mrs Williams is now the minister or deacon in charge.

The evidence of the survey suggests that the issue of the ordination of women to the priesthood will make little difference to the numbers of clergy who will be available for parish work. The poll figure of clergy *objecting* to the move corresponds very accurately with the vote in the General Synod. However, of those who object, the number who will take the road of the former Bishop of London, Graham Leonard, and others and move to Rome is very small. If 5 per cent of the clergy decide to take the financial package on offer and resign their Anglican orders, it would make no difference; their places would quickly be filled by women waiting in the wings to be ordained. In fact, in February 1993 it was reported that more than 500 clergy had asked about the compensation arrangements for those opposed to women priests who intended to leave the ministry. This represents some 5 per cent of the total number of stipendiary clergy and confirms the figure produced by the survey. However, there is a continuing growth in the number of women deacons that more than balances out the decrease in the number of full-time stipendiary male clergy as a result of this decision and various other factors. The number of men in the parishes went down by 1 per cent in 1991, from 10 480 to 10 375. Over the same period the number of full-time stipendiary women deacons rose by 13 per cent to 674.

Another small indication that the issue of women's ordination matters little to those in the community and others not at the heart of the debate, comes from the church of St Paul's, Clapham, South London. The church's stationery states, 'Vicar: The Reverend Helen Cunliffe, MA.' Officially, she is the parish deacon, but the term the people actually use when addressing her is vicar. Ideally, wrote Betty Saunders in her *Church Times* profile of Helen Cunliffe in October 1992, the parish would like *her* to be their priest and not have to import a male priest from somewhere else for every Communion service. When the parish was asked if it would accept a woman in charge, Helen Cunliffe tells of how one woman came back from her holiday especially to vote against it, but she now has stories to tell of people coming round to the idea of having a woman running the parish.

> I remember one woman who was very bitterly opposed and angry. Then my son Edward was born soon after I had been ordained and she came to see the baby. Tight-lipped, she said: 'If I'd been your age I'd have done exactly what you are doing now.' There was frustration, because she had only done menial tasks.

People who objected to the idea have drifted away, which they are able to do because the parish is an urban one.

Once Helen Cunliffe used the reserved sacrament at the Eucharist, but she prefers not to; she looks forward to a time when she will be a priest and everything in the parish will be normal. On the subject of having a woman as the vicar of

St Paul's sacrosanct, a Jamaican granny called Ivy has the best line: 'I give it no thought, God's will be done.'

The Reverend Eileen Lake, who is a hospital chaplain in East London, who I met in the course of making a film for television in 1992, said then that she felt the church's work was being held back by those who were standing in the way of the ordination of women to the priesthood.

> What is being held back is the work of trying to make people outside church life see that there is something about the church that is attractive and that there is something of God in the world. Here we are in what is called the Decade of Evangelism and what is the message we are sending out to the people outside, who we're trying to bring the gospel to?
>
> Very few people on the outside of the church have hang-ups or fears about the ordination of women to the priesthood. Certainly, by reactions that I get in my ministry from people, lots of people who I've spoken to who aren't connected with the church can't understand why it is that women can't be priests; they can do things in other jobs but not in the church. Certainly in the church it is supposed to be talking about men and women being equal.

The survey asked the following question of clergy: 'Are you a supporter of the proposals for the ordination of women to the priesthood as passed by the General Synod and interpreted by the House of bishops?' Of clergy who answered, 66 per cent said 'yes', 25 per cent replied 'no', leaving 8 per cent undecided, and just 4 parish clergy who refused to answer the question. A few hedged their bets by saying, yes, they were in favour in principle, but that now was not the right moment, or that the actual legislation was wrong. Among the clergy without doubt, the issue has raised their blood pressure.

In the General Synod in 1992, the votes were cast in the following proportions:

The Ordination of Women

Houses	For	Against
Bishops	39 (75%)	13 (25%)
Clergy	176 (70.4%)	74 (29.6%)
Laity	169 (67.3%)	82 (32.7%)
Overall	*69.4%*	*30.6%*

The clergy's voting figures on this occasion tally with the survey's findings—a fact that enables me to have confidence in the other findings of the clergy poll. Some of the additional comments from the clergy polled are therefore worth mentioning here.

One vicar, who described himself as a sacramentalist, was not a supporter of the ordination of women, but accepted the Synod's decision and said that 'there has been so much stupidity over this issue and so much lack of Christian charity that the Church of England deserves what it gets.'

A clergyman from a small, rural parish in Sheffield said, 'I prayed with members of my congregation that the vote of God might be made known through the vote of the Synod. I therefore accept it whether I like it or not.' This approach was entirely contradicted by the rector of two small, rural parishes in Suffolk, who described himself as a prayer-book Catholic, and said 'the Synod is bringing quite unnecessary changes and is assuming divine power.'

Having introduced the subject, the next question asked was whether the respondent was taking any active steps to leave the Church of England over the issue of the ordination of women to the priesthood. Here only 4 per cent said that they were taking such steps. If this is an accurate reflection, this sum, multiplied up, is well below the thousand clergy who are, it is said, going to leave the Church of England. However, it should be pointed out that another 5 per cent of the clergy did not answer the question at all. Of those who were *not* taking steps to leave, however, 15 per cent said that they would be expecting to take part in one of the alternative schemes currently being proposed within the

Church of England to accommodate those who were opposed to the ordination of women to the priesthood. This question was asked and the answer given before the Bishop of London floated his diocesan proposals in May to allow clergy taking opposite views to live in parallel with each other in the diocese.

When the clergy were asked if they would have any objection to working alongside a woman priest, 18 per cent said that they would. The implication of this is that there is a reasonably sized group of clergy opposed to the ordination of women to the priesthood who still would, nevertheless, be prepared to have a woman priest as a colleague. Further, 16 per cent of clergy said that they would not accept Communion from a woman priest, although two clergy said that it would depend on whether or not she had celebrated the Eucharist. Another respondent, this time from Exeter, said, 'I already accept Communion from women deacons, the question is badly phrased. If you mean if she had presided at the Eucharist, then the answer is no.'

It would appear, therefore, that there are degrees of opposition to the ordination of women to the priesthood. While 25 per cent of clergy were opposed, only 4 per cent would leave the church because of this issue, and, in between these two camps, was a group of clergy that, although opposed to ordination, would be prepared to work alongside a priest who was a woman or receive Communion from her.

It can be argued that objections to the ordination of women to the priesthood are based mainly on gut feeling and emotion. These emotions have evolved from an individual's own upbringing, cultural experiences or in some cases unresolved sexual difficulties. But opposition to the ordination of women is seldom ever expressed in those terms. Opponents quote biblical precedence, talk of Christ only selecting men to be his apostles. Others talk in terms of church tradition, that for 2000 years the church has accepted that only men may be priests and so, by definition, only men can be priests. As the debate is continued, and certainly since the Synod's vote was taken, these arguments have been heard less and less.

What is now emerging is the argument that it is all a question of authority. The Church of England's Synod, it is felt, does not have the right to overturn tradition, particularly as the Church of England is part of the holy, apostolic and catholic church. It is said that the Church of England does not have the right or authority to take a unilateral decision.

Initially, supporters of the ordination of women countered the earlier arguments with arguments of their own. It was pointed out that Christ only chose Jews as his disciples, so, logically then, this would mean only Jews should become priests. It was also pointed out that the early church did, in fact, have women priests and archival and archeological evidence has backed this up. The final objection with regard to authority is expected to resolve itself, as, with the growing movement in favour of the ordination of women within the Roman Catholic church, too, it is easy to be of the view that the Christian church as a whole is undergoing one of its major sea-changes and that, after a generation or two, the all-male priesthood will have been superseded by a priesthood that is open to both genders. Historians looking back might well see the decision by the Church of England's General Synod as being merely one step in this direction, that the Church of England was moving rather more slowly than some other parts of the Anglican Communion, but a little quicker than the Roman Catholic church. Nevertheless, at least all sections of the Catholic church are moving in the same direction.

Indeed, by the time the rear-guard action was being fought in February 1993 against the Synods' position, little mention was made of any of the theological arguments, but the ground had shifted to discussions about the novel arrangement that had been devised in order to enable the reservations of those who were opposed to being absorbed.

There appears to me to be little evidence to suggest that, should the Church of England be staffed by both men *and* women ordained as priests, it will make any substantial difference to the real issues causing the Church of England to move away from its traditional role. In fact, although there is a minority group amongst the supporters of women's ordination who have experimented with feminist theology to the extent that they have rewritten liturgy to remove sexist language and introduced the idea of God as the mother figure, by and large, if the experience of the Church of Scotland is anything to go by, the presence of a substantial number of women as paid ministers has made little difference to the overall trends. These trends continue as before, with the Church of England, especially in urban and suburban areas, losing touch with the folk-faith of the country.

Indeed, as an interesting aside, it will be fascinating to see, some time in the future, what happens to those members of the Church of England who move over to Rome, arguing not on theological grounds or even admitting to any problems in coming to terms with their own sexuality, but strongly stating that the reason they feel the Church of England's Synod overstepped its authority in making its decision is that it is stepping out of the mainstream of the catholic tradition. What, then, will happen when the Roman Catholic church *also* decides to make a change? This may not happen for another generation, but what is a generation within the huge time-scale of Christendom?

The first Anglican woman to be ordained was Florence Tim Oi Li, ordained in war-torn China in extraordinary circumstances in 1944 when Bishop R. O. Hall took it on himself to ordain her 'a priest in the Church of God.' It is interesting to note that in similarly extraordinary circumstances in Czechoslovakia, when it was under Communist rule, a bishop in the Clandestine Roman Catholic church, it is being suggested, ordained a woman to be his vicar general. All that is necessary in the Roman Catholic church is for a pope to be appointed who is more liberal than the present Pope, John Paul II, who sees the pressing need for priests around the world and decides that the ordination of women is the only solution. He may draw on the precedent from Czechoslovakia and also demonstrate, from the Vatican's own archives, that, certainly in the early centuries of Christianity women were accepted to the priesthood.

To return, though, to the present. There is a danger in the Church of England that the continuing debate about the ordination of women to the priesthood will mask deeper issues. It will be the topic that will grab the attention of the media right up until the first woman is ordained and beyond as women take roles of responsibility in the church. The debate will still be current when the day arrives for a woman bishop to be appointed, or a dean. As the debate rages in the public domain, in contrast, in the privacy of the parishes, life will continue much as before: the churches will become increasingly unfamiliar to the nominal Anglicans, the new liturgies will become consolidated and the old prayer-book forgotten. The urban ways will move into the rural areas and there, too, the committed will presume their interpretation of faith is the one and only truth, and ensure that only committed others join them, on their own terms.

Western society certainly accepts a wider role for women in all spheres of life than it did just one hundred years ago. Then, it would have been inconceivable that women would ever be doctors, surgeons, prime ministers. Maybe one hundred years from now, a future generation will find it hard to understand how the priesthood was ever restricted only to men. It can be argued, therefore, that the controversy in the church is one that is destined to be short-lived and that even if 10 per cent of the church splits away, within a generation or two the rift will have healed naturally, leaving, possibly, only a small rump of misogynists or a traditionalist sect behind that will itself die out or turn into a museum piece in due course. Nevertheless, the fears expressed by Mr Gummer will remain—that the church will cease to be a national church—but for reasons other than those which he proposes.

7
A Church for the 'Unchurched'

It was once said that if you put eight economists into one room and asked them to contemplate ways to tackle the economic problems of the nation, after a while they would come up with nine different solutions. In much the same way, to give a survey of almost 300 clergy an open-ended question and give them the opportunity to get a wide range of concerns and complaints off their chests meant that inevitably the thoughts offered about the future of the Church of England were going to be broad and diverse. This is because every ministry and every parish is unique. The letter below, first published in the *Church of England Newspaper* in June 1991, was sent to me by its author. He lives and works on a housing estate and his daily experience is far, far removed from a rural Anglican idyll.

Life has never been easy, but, during the last twelve months, things have deteriorated rapidly. There has been a marked increase in vandalism, not only destruction to public property but also attacks on people's homes. Burglary, or attempted burglary, has reached epidemic proportions.

Drugs are readily available. Robbery is attempted on the street quite openly. Very young children are sometimes involved, when they move in the circles of older children. Residents are angry but in despair. Local schools are under siege, they have long since run out of money to repair windows.

A Church for the 'Unchurched'

In the Decade of Evangelism, I have been asking myself 'what would be the good news' for the majority of
the people here? Good news would involve release from
fear: fear that one's home will be burgled, fear for one's
children, fear for the elderly who can't defend themselves, fear for the future and where on earth it is all
leading to.

To hold up one's hand in despair . . . seems tanta-
mount to saying that our theology is bankrupt. We have
the advantage of being there to begin to find some answers. There are pressing questions. What is good news
for the vandal? What is good news for the lone parent, in
debt and in drudgery and not coping? What is good news
for the 21 year old who has never worked?

He concluded this letter with a description of 'masses of
people in our nation who feel completely abandoned in the
darkness.' It is interesting that he chooses the same meta-
phor that General Booth did one hundred years ago when
he wrote his major work *In Darkest England: the Way Out*.

Another respondent queried the assumptions of the questionnaire. His parish, he said, is two thirds Muslim, so for
him weddings only happen once a year. Others replied
very differently, talking of writing from a rural viewpoint
and multiparish life, working within a collaborative group
ministry.

There was clearly an enthusiasm for the future amongst
many, particularly those in thriving churches. One, a liberal
Catholic from Sussex said:

I am enthusiastic about the future, there is a new open-
ness and honesty. While it will repel those who wish to
see the church remain static, it opens up new pos-
sibilities for mission and discovery. The church may well
be pushed more to the fringes of society, more lay involvement, more opportunity for self-expression in liturgy, more getting alongside people rather than
remaining aloof.

From Halifax, though, came the view that the Church of England will become more confessional and *less* communal. A priest from an urban parish in Essex called for fewer clergy and more lay leadership, saying that only churches committed to mission and growth will survive: 'The signs appear to be that the Church of England has served its purpose. Perhaps the Almighty has other things in store.'

The parish system, which is at the root of the Church of England's role of being there for everybody, including the 'unchurched', came under attack. Parish boundaries were described as 'meaningless to most people and wasteful of clergy time and resources.' One respondent called for the abolition of clergy freehold and the obligation to live on the job. He supported getting rid of many of the old and poor-quality church buildings. Yet, such views were countered by a liberal Evangelical from a suburban parish in Cambridge, who said that he feared for the Church of England because it was becoming more sectarian. He hoped that the church would find new ways of serving the *whole* community in Christ's name, not just the congregation. More typical, though, was the comment of a priest with a suburban ministry in Surrey who thought that the church had gone 'too far down the line of trying to be a church that can accommodate everyone. If we try we are in danger of losing our identity.'

There is certainly an acceptance of a general need for there to be a tightening up on discipline with regard to baptism, confirmation, and marriage after divorce and to adopt rules that are consistent across the board. An evangelical from rural Staffordshire, for example, said that he was of the opinion that we ought to 'cease to offer a service of marriage to everyone, this would resolve the problem of marrying divorced people in church. I feel that we will find that the Church of England becomes less accepted in the community as the state church and this will have a good and a bad side to it.'

Taking the views of the clergy surveyed, the split between those who felt the church's first priority should be to

114

the 'unchurched', and those who felt priority should be given to building up the Christian community was striking. From a rural parish in Devon came the view:

> There is a great need to become a more missionary church. The church is only very slowly recognizing this. Present policy on baptisms and weddings needs amending, but looks as though this will take much time. There is also in my parish a great interest in the spiritual side of life, but scepticism about the Church of England. Development of prayer, meditation and so on, as opposed to liturgical services will be important.

Yet as the Anglo-Catholic from Wiltshire quoted earlier, said:

> I believe the Church of England must stand by the parish system, i.e. to have a personal relationship and commitment to all who reside in these islands who are not otherwise committed. We are not a sect or congregational set up and must not for reasons of convenience or financial difficulty or supposed lack of vocations become one either.

A charismatic evangelical from an urban parish on Merseyside welcomes the present Archbishop of Canterbury as the best thing to have happened to the Church of England in his memory! 'The charismatic movement', he said, 'is the key to the future; churches which define themselves in terms of the past have no future.' Also, a Catholic from rural Norfolk observes:

> the Church of England may well disappear into a complete realignment of Christians in this country. The new divisions will be between the liberals who 'make it up as they go along' and those who hold the faith handed down the ages in trust.

Further, a charismatic evangelical from Essex takes the view that:

it is only really evangelical charismatic parishes that are showing signs of real growth, but we are scorned by others—I have been openly criticized by senior clergy because I have dared to challenge the faithlessness and lack of vision of church leaders. However, God is at work and I see a growing movement of evangelical parishes prepared to church plant and go against the diocesan authorities in order to extend God's kingdom. The parish boundary, formerly sacrosanct, will be crossed more and more as we follow the Holy Spirit's leading, and I see ahead large parishes investing in growth rather than propping up 'dead wood'. There will be a move away from dead traditionalism to Spirit-filled vitality.

There, in a nutshell, is the choice for, as a liberal from a Southampton parish wrote, 'the Church of England is becoming exclusive, which worries me, e.g. funeral service is virtually unusable with non-church people.' This view is reiterated by a radical catholic from inner city Camberwell who observed that most churches are clubs for the like-minded:

This results in a sectarian church increasingly obsessed with its own problems and intoxicated by its own fantasies. Emphasis in biblicism is a flight from both. Homophobia is a serious problem and a sign of fear of the unknown and a backward, waking desire for safe uniformity. But there are wonderful exceptions to all this!

From a rural parish in Kent came an expression of fear: 'I fear fundamentalism at both ends. The evangelical wing's star is rising and the anglo-catholic wing is uncertain where to land.'

Also, from suburban Birmingham came the observation, 'the Church of England is anachronistic, isolated and essentially divisive in its perceptions and identity. The key issue is, is it the church *in* England or the secular church *of* England?'

A Church for the 'Unchurched'

In the same vein, a call came from an inner city parish in York for the Church of England to rediscover its role as the church of England and to disabuse itself of a tendency to sectarianism. This view was backed up by another Anglo-Catholic from Yorkshire who sees the breakdown of the parochial system ahead: 'This would be sad, there is now so much "congregationalism and eclectic worship".' He thought there should be a formal division of the Church of England into traditional and modernistic elements. However, a clergyman who described himself as a liberal Evangelical from Northumberland stated that his main hope is that the church become more inclusive: 'The local church should seek to be a focus for the spiritual aspirations of the whole community. The church should become more celebratory.'

Looking at this from a slightly different angle, a priest from a rural commuter village in the South East of England described the spread of the evangelical influence as being partly beneficial, but the church could cease to be 'Catholic and reformed'. He wrote, 'It faces a possible withdrawal from the role of being the national and established church in the face of "competition" from house churches, independent fellowships, etc.' However, he also said what he would like to see happen: 'the Church of England should try not to let go of the parish system of national coverage. By the use of locally ordained ministers and non-stipendiary ministers it could have a person in every local centre.'

Also on this subject, from the Wirral came the suspicion of one liberal Catholic that Evangelical churches will continue to become stronger. 'I fear this may be associated with an increasingly "closed" attitude towards those outside the church (or even in some cases, those who are not seen as "real Christians" within the church).'

Putting all the views together, as diverse as they are, the survey has gone a long way to confirming my impression that the real split within the Church of England concerns the church's responsibility to those who are *not* members. The

117

clergy accept that changes are taking place rapidly and more are to come. Many of the changes to the parish structure are seen not as desirable, but as inevitable because of financial restraints. A common feeling, too, is that the pattern of the stipendiary ministry will change substantially and new lay authority to celebrate Communion will need to be given or new non-stipendiary clergy will need to be ordained. There is also a general lack of confidence in the leadership, particularly that of the bishops.

So, there is a collective feel that the present Church of England is under pressure, both financially and socially. Many of the clergy polled think that this is no bad thing and that the church will be forced to concentrate on its role as a Christian missionary organization in a pagan society. It will need to regroup, retrench, and discard its role of being a point of spiritual contact for the 'unchurched'. Others think this is the very *worst* thing to do and that, using as many alternative forms of ministry as possible, the church should maintain its role as the church of all the nation for as long as possible.

The split away from the Church of England on the part of a few, unhappy with the ordination of women, is considered a minor affair. The major split is between those who believe that the Church of England should rejoice in becoming a Christian denomination and those who fear that this must be prevented, that the church should retain its position as the institution dedicated to the spiritual well-being of all, including, and perhaps especially, those who are not regular members, the great 'unchurched'.

The debate, therefore, comes down to the issue of exclusivity versus availability. It is to do with the psychology of the church: whether the Church of England believes that it is chosen by God and in a uniquely righteous position, with unique access to God and his truth, and at odds with a pagan world, or whether it is a church that keeps the rumour of God alive and has the humility to accept that it has a truth but is still open to mystery and doubt, though, nevertheless, exists to enable the 'unchurched' to capture their own brief glimpses of the eternal by being there to serve at times of need or to co-celebrate in times of rejoicing. However, this wider availability can still exist even if the church sheds its establishment role in which it is seen by the wider world to give authority to the wider world's activities.

The question of disestablishment does not simply involve, on the one hand, the Church of England being there for the whole nation, representing the nation's tribal traditions and enduing or endowing the monarch and government with authority, or, on the other hand, being the church pure and untainted by the world, living in spiritual isolation, concerned only with the salvation of the few. There *is* a middle road, and that is of the humble church working for the benefit of all, to meet spiritual, and often social, needs, not because it has a monopoly on spiritual truth, but because it is an enabling force, a way through which ordinary people can gain some access to that truth. It exists to enable individuals to find their own way as well as providing corporate means by which groups can come together for special purposes.

Similar questions to these now being asked about the church in Britain have, for many years, been asked about missionary work abroad. Indeed, these questions can be seen to be relevant in both contexts if the Church of England is regarded as being a missionary organization in a pagan land. When reviewing the book *The Celtic Way* by Doctor Ian Bradley, John Pearce wrote in the *Church of England Newspaper* in March 1993 about the Celtic church and its baptizing of the pagan into Christianity with such a view in mind and so his comments are relevant here.

The question is always whether adoption of pagan customs actually compromises the Christian faith. All this is very relevant to the discussion which is now going on about the work of overseas missions and how indigenous is the Christianity which we have planted.

At the last World Council of Churches assembly there was major controversy when one lecturer introduced elements from non-Christian religion into the beginning of her address. We are always in danger of transferring our superficial cultural conventions as if they were an essential part of the gospel and nowhere has this been more truly the case than in the inner city ministries of England. This book therefore raises all kinds of interesting issues.

If one can stand back for a moment and see our own British traditions and customs as an outside anthropologist might, the meaning of such a view becomes clearer.

I said earlier that this book was particularly written with the 'unchurched' in mind and that enthusiasts would look after themselves. This, I believe, will be the case, but there will be some circumstances in which the interests of the enthusiasts and those of the 'unchurched' may come into conflict.

One possible area of conflict concerns church planting, which is when small teams from a highly successful church head out into the community to plant the seeds of another church where they feel there is a need. Sometimes this is done by enthusiasts from outside the community coming to what they perceive as a derelict congregation, joining up, joining the parochial church council, becoming activists and, depending on your perspective, revitalizing or hijacking the congregation. In these circumstances a local body of folk attached to the building and their own traditions can feel marginalized and excluded. Resentment can result. This is not a major problem as church planting normally takes place within an urban setting, so the church buildings concerned are not built on the sacred places of old and the members of the congregation do not generally have deep roots in the area that go back generations. However, exclusive congregations can make newcomers feel very uncomfortable. Initially, the new, vibrant Evangelicals will appear very welcoming, full of smiles, almost using the techniques identified as 'love bombing' that are adopted by a number of sects. If newcomers question anything, however, do not fit into the mould, are too liberal in theological thought, and too questioning of what they are told, that welcome will wear very thin.

One major problem that results is that the more exclusive congregations become, the more they move away from what is recognized as Anglican and they take on their own brands of theological enthusiasm. This problem was highlighted at a recent conference on Anglican church planting held at Holy Trinity, Brompton in London, when it was suggested that the new, 'enthusiastic' churches sometimes strayed from the basic Anglicanism from which they derived their authority. Indeed, the Bishop of Southwell said that the new Anglican plants required 'authorized worship leaders and a recognized form of worship. If it doesn't have an *Anglican* ethos, it is going to have some *other* sort of ethos.' However, in London over the last 20 years, there have been 200 church plants, a quarter of them outside parish boundaries; in only 4 cases have there been problems.

At the conference, the Bishop of London made an appeal to those planning the planting of a new church to be patient with church structures: 'I get just as impatient with the structures as anyone else. By patient, collaborative work, you will get there.'

An extra, small point. The fact that such a high proportion of planted churches in London have strayed over parish boundaries is a further indication that, in urban areas in particular, the parish boundaries have to be redrawn.

There are other potential points of contact between the 'unchurched' and the Christian gospel, though, that do not involve an individual seeking out a congregation to join. These are opportunities for people to become passive rather than proactive members of the church. They include the contacts with religious ideas that result from religious education in schools and the glimpses of faith people have through the mass media. As important as these areas are, however, they fall outside the scope of both the survey and this book.

Another area of conflict produces stronger feelings. If there is hostility in the church towards meeting the needs of the folk-faith of the nation, there is even more hostility towards moves the church is making towards collaborating with those of other faiths. In February 1993, the General Synod's board of mission produced a report, 'Multifaith Worship?' It strongly advised that multifaith services should take place in non-religious buildings to avoid the difficulties posed by using a specific Christian place of worship. The response of the Reverend Tony Higton, founder of Action for Biblical Witness to Our Nation, and a member of the General Synod, was to take issue with the guidelines proposed by the report. He thinks that they fail to deal with 'the false teaching of justification by works inevitably implied by multifaith adoption.' He says, too, that the document is weak on the issue of idolatry. The multifaith service which has received the greatest criticism has been that of the commonwealth observants in Westminster Abbey. The Abbey, being at the centre of the folk-faith of the nation as well as being a place of Christian worship, is directly under the control of the Queen, who is, of course, monarch to those of all religions on the island. The Dean, the Very Reverend Michael Mayne, reacted to the report by saying:

> the Abbey is a place dedicated to Christian worship for 900 years and it will be clear to all present that the observation has Christian orientation to this place. That the commonwealth is a community of nations in which other great and historic faiths have an honoured place. We are very glad to have with us representatives of those faiths who will be taking part in this observance so far as they feel able to do so.

When it comes to co-operative ventures between Anglican parishes and other Christian churches and denominations, the survey suggested that the more exclusive the congregation, the less inclined it was to experiment ecumenically. The fact, too, that in rural areas, opportunities for Anglicans, Roman Catholics and free church members to collaborate on any regular basis are restricted by geography, meant that any evidence from the survey of real Christian unity was scant. Indeed, at parish level, the Church of England does not seem to be taking ecumenism very seriously at all. When asked if they had regular meetings with Roman Catholic and free church clergy in the area, 75 per cent of those surveyed said that they do but only 14 per cent said that that meeting is every week, and 78 respondents said the meeting is only once a month, with 61 saying meetings are even less frequent, ranging from once every 2 months to once a quarter. One clergyman from a rural parish of Worcester dismissed such meetings as not being very relevant. A radical Evangelical from Warrington said that he meets once a month with those of other denominations, but this is a recent innovation. A clergyman from Devon volunteered that he had held meetings regularly previously, but does not see any way forward as yet. In suburban Bromley, Kent, meetings are just beginning again. Only one of all the clergy who replied, that is, only one in nearly 300, has a daily meeting with those of other churches and denominations, and this is because he is a member of a local ecumenical project in his town in Warwickshire.

When it came to holding regular services with congregations outside the Anglican church, 64 per cent of the clergy said that they do. 'We try to cater for people as Christians', wrote one respondent from Northumberland. Yet, a priest working in a rural mining community said that holding these services is 'deadly!'

To leave ecumenical issues aside however and return to the question of bridging the gap between an increasingly sectarian Church of England and the 'unchurched' at large, maybe one way forward is for the church to be more open about its own doubts and uncertainties.

It would appear that there is no general hostility to religion or spirituality in the community; it is that there is only a small group, perhaps 10 per cent of the population, that feels it can ascribe to what it perceives to be the set rules, beliefs and dogmas of the church. There are possibly many outside the church who would love to be members of a worshipping community, to identify with the church, to have an active spiritual life, but who feel that it would involve intellectual dishonesty or an uneasy feeling in the conscience resulting from having to squash their questions and what they perceive as doubts, of hiding their uncertainties and fitting themselves into some preconceived Christian mould. The theologian Doctor Elizabeth Templeton wrote of this feeling in an article in the *Church Times* on 30 April 1993: 'huge freedoms can emerge from faith but my concern is with a more modest freedom, one not enough manifested in our corporate Christian life: the freedom to be truthful with one another with questions of faith.' She tells the story, too, of how, in the early seventies, when teaching theology, she found year after year a trickle of students about to sit final exams and move on to parish ministry wrestling with the question of how they were to emerge from the chrysalis of theological training to be butterflies of confident Orthodoxy.

> For they knew that the gospels were not documentary history; they knew that debates about the creed were sometimes won or lost by bishops missing ferry boats; they knew that, if you said it was the hand of God that delayed ferry boats, you had problems about where the hand of God was in the Zeebrugge disaster. But they felt a terrible, looming, unvoiced pressure that the move from classroom to pulpit involved them in hiding all that, certainly from their people, and if possible from themselves.

On one occasion, confronting a group of young ministers, she found that the room divided into those who said that no candidate for ministry ought to have major questions about faith and those who acknowledged the entitlement to question. All, with the exception of two men, however, believed that there should be no public admission among congregational office bearers that such an unfinished agenda existed for a clergyman.

Doctor Templeton went on to say that she received correspondence as the Editor of *Trust* which now filled many box files.

> Over and over again people describe their frustration and furtiveness about having doubts they have to sit on, questions they feel would be ostracized, opinions they know to be officially heterodox.
>
> I am sure we are weakened as a truthful, truth-seeking body by the sense that we must affirm the 'biblical faith' or 'apostolic faith' as if these were incontrovertible data. Certainly we inherit all that to wrestle with; but without candour about how properly hard it is to affirm it, unqualified, in the light of twentieth-century cultural awareness, we will create a situation in which embarrassed lip-service is paid to doctrines that people no longer live inside. If people do, as some clearly do, happily and confidently live inside them, they have nothing to fear from the challenge of those who can't . . . the rumours of intellectual dishonesty are too widespread to be contained by authoritarian pronouncement.
>
> Wrestling for the truth is not shameful, nor impious, nor malevolent. It seems to me to be faithful to Jacob struggling at Peniel to elicit God's name.

I would add only one observation to those of Doctor Templeton. The 'unchurched', the occasional churchgoers, and all struggling to understand the meaning of life, to 'know the name of God' in this most complicated age, would greatly welcome the knowledge that church members, too, are fellow travellers in this, not people who have found a 'Never never land' and to which they will only admit others on their own strict terms.

It was the Archbishop of Canterbury, speaking in July 1993, who found an apt image to describe the type of church he wished to see that would not alienate the people on the edges. He said that, on a visit to Papua New Guinea, he had visited a cathedral that had a roof but no walls. People were able to come in or hover around the edges, listening for a while if they wished, and then walk away.

> I believe with all my heart that the Church of Jesus Christ should be a church of blurred edges . . . a church of no walls where people can ask their hardest questions without condemnation and share their deepest fear without reproach.

Appendix: The Results of the Questionnaire

A total of 500 clergy serving in parishes in England were contacted, each by individual letter, and asked if they would complete a questionnaire the results of which would be used in this book. It was open to all clergy to reply anonymously if they wished.

The clergy were chosen at random from *Crockford's Clerical Directory* and 311 replies were received, a response rate of 62 per cent. Of those responding, a number had very recently retired or declined, for other reasons, to fill in all of the detailed questionnaire, but, nevertheless, sent some parish information. Thus, the results of the survey are based on 282 replies (56 per cent).

Of those polled, 16 per cent said that they were a member of a team ministry. Of those who were not, 27 per cent were assisted by a curate, 12 per cent by a non-stipendiary minister and 20 per cent received regular help from a retired clergyman, and 46 per cent from a reader.

PARISH PROFILE

How many parishes are you responsible for?

66 per cent are responsible for 1 parish.
16 per cent for 2 parishes.
6 per cent for 3 parishes.
3 per cent for 4 parishes.
4 per cent for 5 parishes.
1 per cent for 6 parishes.
1 per cent for 7 parishes.
3 per cent did not answer.

How many church buildings are you or your team responsible for?

The average reply was 2.

35 per cent of buildings are over 501 years old.

30 per cent of buildings are between 101 and 200 years old.

25 per cent of buildings are 100 years old or less.

10 per cent of buildings are between 201 and 500 years old.

What description best fits your area of ministry?

31 per cent replied 'rural'.

20 per cent replied 'suburban'.

17 per cent replied 'urban'.

13 per cent replied 'rural town'.

7 per cent replied 'inner city'.

(Others are mixed geographical areas.)

What is the civil population?

25 155 is the average for 'inner city'.

12 596 is the average for 'suburban'.

11 303 is the average for 'urban'.

8626 is the average for 'rural town'.

2109 is the average for 'rural'.

What is the size of the electoral roll?

285 is the average for 'rural town'.

271 is the average for 'suburban'.

188 is the average for 'rural'.

171 is the average for 'urban'.

118 is the average for 'inner city'.

What is the average Sunday attendance?

208 is the average for 'rural town' (2.4 per cent of average civil population).

183 is the average for 'suburban' (1.5 per cent of average civil population).

134 is the average for 'urban' (1.2 per cent of average civil population).

119 is the average for 'inner city' (0.5 per cent of average civil population).

83 is the average for 'rural' (3.9 per cent of average civil population).

Which service attracts the most people in the course of a year?

69 per cent replied that the main Christmas service is the most popular (outright or equally with another).

17 per cent replied that the Easter service is the most popular (outright or equally with another).

10 per cent replied that the harvest festival is the most popular (outright or equally with another).

12 per cent replied that the Remembrance Day service is the most popular (outright or equally with another).

Other replies included a holiday service, big funerals, Mothering Sunday, church parades, and a church/school anniversary service.

WORSHIP AND MINISTRY

In numerical terms, are the congregations in the churches for which you are responsible increasing, decreasing, or static?

49.5 per cent increasing.

38.5 per cent static.

4 per cent decreasing.

8 per cent did not answer the question.

On average, each Sunday, how many services of Holy Communion do you celebrate according to ASB Rite A?

44 per cent said 1 service.

22 per cent said 2 services.

7 per cent said 3 services.

1 per cent said 4 services.

26 per cent of clergy did not answer or did not celebrate according to this Rite.

How many do you celebrate according to ASB Rite B?

18 per cent said 1 service.

5 per cent said 2 services.

1 per cent said 3 or 4 services.

76 per cent did not answer or did not celebrate according to this Rite.

How many do you celebrate according to the Book of Common Prayer?

38 per cent said 1 service.
8 per cent said 2 services.
1 per cent said 3 services.
1 per cent said 4 services.
52 per cent did not answer or did not celebrate according to this Rite.

How many do you celebrate according to local variations?

9 per cent said 1 service.
2 per cent said 2 services.
1 per cent said 3 services.
88 per cent did not answer or did not celebrate using local variations.

Of all celebrations of Holy Communion:

50 per cent are celebrated according to Rite A.
27 per cent are celebrated according to the Book of Common Prayer.
12 per cent are celebrated according to Rite B.
11 per cent are celebrated according to local combinations of all.

The sign of peace

84 per cent of clergy responding said that a sign of the peace was exchanged at one or more of the Holy Communion services celebrated on a Sunday.

Which form of the Holy Communion service do you prefer to celebrate?

71 per cent said ASB Rite A.
4 per cent said ASB Rite B.
6 per cent said Book of Common Prayer.
The others prefer local variations or did not answer.

Which form of service do you normally use for baptisms?

84 per cent use the service in the ASB.
2 per cent use the Book of Common Prayer.
11 per cent use local variations of the set services.
3 per cent did not answer.

Do baptisms usually take place in the course of the main Sunday service?

58 per cent said yes.
29 per cent said no.
13 per cent did not answer.

What is your policy towards baptizing children of non-churchgoers?

32 per cent always baptize a child.
63 per cent baptize a child only after preparation.
2 per cent refuse baptizm until the parents attend church regularly.
3 per cent did not answer.

Which form of service do you normally use to conduct funerals?

62 per cent use the service in the ASB.
11 per cent use the Book of Common Prayer.
22 per cent use local variations of the set services.
5 per cent did not answer

Which form of service do you normally use to conduct weddings?

72 per cent use the service in the ASB.
7 per cent use the Book of Common Prayer.
16 per cent use local variations of the set services.
5 per cent did not answer

Have you formally asked your parish for one day off per week?

44 per cent said yes.
50 per cent said no.
6 per cent did not answer.

How many parishioners did you visit last week at their home or in hospital?

11 was the average number visited, of which an average of 61 per cent were regular churchgoers.

Do you feel the quota system is a fair method of raising diocesan and central church funds?

79 per cent said yes.
15 per cent said no.
6 per cent did not answer.

Are the faculty regulations relating to changes in the fabric of the church acceptable, need tightening, too strict?

68 per cent think they are acceptable.
1 per cent think they need tightening.
27 per cent think they are too strict.
4 per cent did not answer.

ECUMENICAL RELATIONS

Do you have regular meetings with the Roman Catholic and free church clergy in the area?

75 per cent said yes.
23 per cent said no.
2 per cent did not answer.

Of those who replied yes:

51 per cent meet monthly.
23 per cent meet every 2 months
17 per cent meet quarterly.
9 per cent meet every week.

Do you hold regular services with other churches or denominations?

64 per cent said yes.
33 per cent said no.
3 per cent did not answer.

Appendix

Do you share a building or facilities with another church or denomination?

12 per cent said yes.
85 per cent said no.
3 per cent did not answer.

THE CHURCH TODAY

Are you a supporter of the proposals for the ordination of women to the priesthood as passed by the General Synod and interpreted by the House of Bishops?

66 per cent said yes.
25 per cent said no.
8 per cent don't know.
1 per cent did not answer.

Are you taking any active steps to leave the Church of England on the issue of the ordination of women to the priesthood?

4 per cent said yes.
91 per cent said no.
5 per cent did not answer.

Would you be expecting to take part in any of the alternative schemes currently being proposed within the Church of England to accommodate those who are opposed to the ordination of women to the priesthood?

15 per cent said yes.
62 per cent said no.
3 per cent don't know.
20 per cent did not answer.

Would you have any objection to working alongside a woman priest?

18 per cent said yes.
77 per cent said no.
2 per cent don't know.
3 per cent did not answer.

Would you accept Communion from a woman priest?

79 per cent said yes.

16 per cent said no.

2 per cent don't know.

3 per cent did not answer.

Do you believe the monarch should continue to be the supreme governor of the Church of England?

53 per cent said yes.

36 per cent said no.

2 per cent don't know.

9 per cent did not answer.

Would you favour the disestablishment of the Church of England?

39 per cent said yes.

50 per cent said no.

2 per cent don't know.

9 per cent did not answer.

Would you, as permitted, be prepared to marry couples where one is or both are divorced?

61 per cent said yes.

32 per cent said no.

7 per cent did not answer.

Would you if permitted be prepared to conduct a service of blessing for a homosexual couple?

14 per cent said yes.

76 per cent said no.

3 per cent don't know.

7 per cent did not answer.

PERSONAL

What is your age?

33 per cent of the clergy polled are in their 40s.

31 per cent in their 50s.

16 per cent in their 60s.

15 per cent in their 30s.
1 per cent in their 70s.
4 per cent did not answer.

When were you ordained a deacon?

33 per cent were ordained in the 1980s.
28 per cent in the 1960s.
24 per cent in the 1970s.
9 per cent in the 1950s.
1 per cent in the 1940s.
1 per cent in the 1990s.
4 per cent did not answer.

Do you have any other professional or vocational qualifications?

58 per cent said yes.
39 per cent said no.
3 per cent did not answer.

How are you normally addressed by members of the congregation?

80 per cent by their Christian name.
7 per cent as Mr . . .
25 per cent by a formal title, such as Vicar or Canon.
14 per cent as Father or Father . . .
From these results it will be seen that some clergy normally expect to be addressed in more than one style. Unusual responses included 'Oi you!', 'Friar', 'Padre' or 'Pip's Daddy' (Pip being a dog).

What is your marital status?

85 per cent are married.
10 per cent are single.
5 per cent are either divorced, separated, widowed, or did not answer.

If married, does your spouse share your faith?

84 per cent said yes.
1 per cent said no.
1 per cent don't know.

14 per cent did not answer.

Is your spouse involved in parish work?

68 per cent said yes.
16 per cent said no.
16 per cent did not answer.

Is your spouse in paid employment?

50 per cent said yes.
35 per cent said no.
15 per cent did not answer.
(21.3 per cent wives work as teachers.)

75 per cent of clergy contacted who said they had children aged 15 or over said that their children shared their faith. 86 per cent of the children had been confirmed.

Have you ever regretted seeking ordination?

17 per cent said yes.
79 per cent said no.
4 per cent did not answer.

Would you like to leave parish ministry if the opportunity arose?

15 per cent said yes.
66 per cent said no.
2 per cent don't know.
17 per cent did not answer.

Have you ever prayed or spoken in tongues?

28 per cent said yes.
68 per cent said no.
4 per cent did not answer.

Do you make a regular confession on a personal basis to a fellow priest?

25 per cent said yes.
70 per cent said no.
5 per cent did not answer.

Books Used for Further Reading

John Barton and John Halliburton, *Believing in the Church*. SPCK 1981.

Ian Bradley, *The Celtic Way*. Darton, Longman & Todd 1993.

Jack Burton, *The Gap*. Triangle 1991.

Douglas Davies, Charles Watkins and Michael Winter, *Church and Religion in Rural England*. T. & T. Clark 1991.

Leslie Francis, *Rural Anglicanism*. Collins 1985.

Robin Gill, *The Myth of the Empty Church*. SPCK 1993.

Peter Hammond, *The Parson in the Victorian Parish*. Hodder & Stoughton 1977.

Henry Mayr-Harting, *The Coming of Christianity to Anglo-Saxon England*. Penguin 1972.

Charles Moore, A. N. Wilson and Gavin Stamp, *The Church in Crisis*. Hodder and Stoughton 1986.

Derry Brabbs and Nigel Nicolson, *English Country Churches*. Weidenfield & Nicolson 1985.

Doctor Robin Rees, *Weary and Ill at Ease*. Gracewing 1993.